Poems

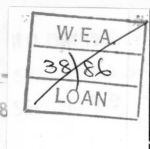

Boris Pasternak

BORIS PASTERNAK [*POEMS*]

translated from the Russian
by Eugene M. Kayden

The University of Michigan Press
Ann Arbor

I Dedicate These Translations
To My Father and Mother,
in Memoriam

Boris Pasternak sent the manuscript of THE PASSING STORM
to Eugene Kayden in appreciation of his work.
This manuscript is reproduced in facsimile
in this volume.

Some of the translations in this volume
have appeared in the following periodicals:
THE NEW STATESMAN AND NATION; THE NEW REPUBLIC;
THE COLORADO QUARTERLY; THE RUSSIAN REVIEW;
THE CHRISTIAN CENTURY.

I had a brief exchange of letters with Boris Leonidovich Pasternak in the summer of 1958, before I had the privilege of reading his novel, *Doctor Zhivago*. From his home in Peredélkino he wrote to me under date of 22 August 1958, a long letter evoked —and, in part, provoked—by a statement of mine that his real home remains poetry where his vision is personal and unique in its intensity. Yet I believe with Mr. Pasternak that the future has taken residence in the streets and byways of the world, that we are part of it, and I am filled with the "silent music of happiness" heard at the heart of his novel and poetry because of my humble submission to the mystery of life and my serene confidence in the dawn of the new dispensation of kindliness and love among men everywhere. I reproduce his letter, written in English, with a few minor excisions unrelated to the issue of his poetry.

"In your last and previous letters, in your short essay on Pushkin, in your translations of his poetry and in your work on my behalf, I do not find anything other than worthy aims and achievements. You say I am 'first and last a poet, a lyric poet.' Is it really so? And should I feel proud of being just that? And do you realize the meaning of my being no more than that, whereas it hurts me to feel that I have not had the ability to express in greater fullness the whole of poetry and life in their complete unity? But what am I without the novel, and what have you to write about me without drawing upon that work, its terms and revelations?

"I cannot say, like Mayakóvsky, let's have 'as many poets as possible, good and various others.' Against mere numbers, I should wish—not literally of course—that poets were few; the matter of their scarcity does not interest me much—but that one poet should be true and great, expressing supremely and inimitably the life of his age. Art is not simply a description of life, but a setting forth of the uniqueness of being. What we call the splendor and vividness of description is not a feature imputed merely to style, but something far greater, namely, the presence of a new conception and the philosophic sense of life's own oneness and wholeness. The significant writer of his epoch (and I want no other beside him) is a revelation, a representation of the unknown, unrepeatable uniqueness of living reality. What else is originality if not a cultural event having its source in the world's absolute total reality?

"Many forgotten periods of history were once thought to be the end of the world, like our present nuclear situation. Each age, each stage of historical existence is compounded of two terms, the known and the unrevealed. The latter is infinite and unknown, because the future is at all times a part of this unexplored and unknown infinity that I can speak of without resort to mysticism—the burgeoning, profound, momentous tomorrow.

"Each art, especially that of poetry, means a great deal more than it comprises. Its essence and values are symbolic. This does in no manner signify that we possess the key by which we can discover behind every word or condition some other hidden sense—mystical, occult, or providential—as was erroneously believed of the dramatic works of Ibsen, Maeterlinck, or Leonid Andréyev. Nor does it mean that each true, creative poetical text ought to be a parable or an allegory. What I want to say is that besides and above the separate tropes and metaphorical turns of a poem there exists a figurative tendency, a drift in the poetry itself and in art as a whole—and that is its chief significance—to relate the general, summary purport of a composition to broader and more fundamental ideas—in order to reveal the sublimity of life and the unfathomable values of human existence. I am tempted to say that art does not equal itself, does not mean itself alone, but that it means tangibly something beyond itself. In this way we call art symbolic in essence.

"If I believe an author is not too great in his natural endowments, or if I do not discover in his works this immense spiritual quality, this sense of all-surpassing, overarching importance to life, he is as nothing to me however good the written page. It is as if somebody began to scurry to and fro in an open field, waving flags and lights along the railway track, without a railway train in sight. Art is for me a manifestation and a symptom; it must show that we stand in the presence of new all-encompassing values, in the presence of the great.

"Beginning with Pushkin we have our Russian contemporaneity, the real and the true, our modern thinking and spiritual consciousness. Pushkin erected the house of our spiritual life, the edifice of Russia's historical awareness. Lermontov was its first tenant. In Lermontov we have the independent confessional note in the subsequent intellectual tradition of our century, in poetry and prose, later enriched by the magnificent concreteness of Leo Tolstoy, then Chekhov's sharp-eyed absolute sensitiveness to reality. But whereas Pushkin is objective, tangible, and just, with generalizations of the widest meaning, Lermontov is passionate and personal, and therefore more limited; whereas Pushkin is realistic and exalted in creative activity, Lermontov is its living personal testimony. And as you have stated it, his operatic romanticism is apparent in part. The influence of Byron was unmistakable, because half of Europe had been under his spell. But what we wrongly take for romanticism in Lermontov seems to me to be in fact the unbalanced nature of this modern personal biographical realism and the foreshadowing of our modern poetry and prose. I dedicated *My Sister Life* not to the memory of Lermontov but to the poet himself as though he were living in our midst—to his spirit still effectual in our literature. What was he to me, you ask, in the summer of 1917?—The personification of creative adventure and discovery, the principle of everyday free poetical statement."

I here allow myself a few comments on Pasternak's vision of poetry, with special reference to Pushkin and Tyutchev. I have in mind his scope and freshness, his spacious seriousness, his personal heroism, and the poetic directness and serenity of his maturer work. As with other great Russian masters of prose and verse, to be an artist is to be intensely religious. Like Tolstoy's his work is infused with the sense of the totality of life, with social compassion and an anti-heroic philosophy of history. In him life draws the deeper breath. His physical objects are unvaryingly dynamic, with the immediacy of the material, and with their spiritual quintessence wonderfully in place, for so much is at stake beyond perceptive technical performance or inviolate lyric grace.

The poet's message, I understand Boris Leonidovich to say, is a special way of apprehension, an act of vision, which, like wisdom, is an act of love and compassion in human destiny. It is not, strictly speaking, an act of moral conversion, social aspiration, and justice, or political exhortation. The poet is unique because he speaks to us as free men with a sense of a revelation, that our sublime vision of life as an end in itself may not perish. His words demand our turning to the future that we may share a life of objective reality and truth. For this reason I have long regarded Mr. Pasternak as the greatest poet to emerge from the Revolution of 1917, as a man with roots deep down in Russia's cultural history, as a poet who has his "fame and partnership in homebred Russian art." I have shunned, in my translations of him, the literal and the neutral; I have preserved what is literary and ripe in contemporary speech; I have not aimed to make my versions faithful to schoolroom notions of cramped accuracy—but faithful to the spirit of Pasternak's vision of life. If I have at times narrowed the compass and delicacy of his lines, failed him in versatility, passion, and lyric loveliness, if I have not reached accuracy, let alone perfection, I have at least lived with his mind and spirit for many years, made his growth my growth, fascinated by the imaginative color of the original and heartened in my timidity by his counsel—the hint of a translator to a translator—to have the courage of imperfection.

Pasternak came in an age of religious and philosophic waywardness, at a time of estrangement between philosophy, science, social statesmanship, and the fine arts, at a time of great crisis, war, revolution, and social division embracing the whole of human life. It was a time when authority was feared or mistrusted, and every claim to absolute understanding under suspicion—the poet's claim in particular, a claim which proves itself only as deeper insight and perception, as a form of love, and as a commitment to freedom in the name of individual worth, in the name of the vision of life that must be worshipped. This was Russia's heritage from the time of Pushkin:

> O Poet, believe not in the crowd's acclaim.
> Soon pass the noontide ecstasies of praise;
> The mob will mock you, fools their judgment raise.
> But live, unmoved, above their storm and blame,
> A king apart. Shine, Poet, in your fame!
> Go, free, in fearlessness, on splendid ways,
> Attaining mastery of thought and phrase,
> And for your noble work no payment claim.
> Your art alone your wage. O highest judge,
> And stern tribunal of your work entire,
> Are you content? Exacting craftsman, say,
> Is art enough? Then let the rabble grudge,
> And curse, and spit upon your altar fire,
> And shake your tripod in their childish play.

The poet's word is a revelation of the Eternal. This is Pasternak's meaning when he speaks of the art of Pushkin as "objective, tangible, and just" and as a poetic act "exalted in creative activity." Indeed, the poet is of this world and of the obdurate earth, a neighbor among neighbors, the closest of man's neighbors even in his aloofness. But the function of the poet is greater by far than the ways of nature, welfare, knowledge, and social progress. His intimations are not ordinary. His perceptions are unique and integral. But if he possesses no steady vision of reality he runs the hazard of brutish passivity, ambiguous impressionism, pointless rebellion, or destructive cynicism. He is then a disinherited spirit, the least in the world of men, as Pushkin has truly said, a man who has diminished himself.

No! The Poet's way is the way of insight, love, and revelation as the art of profoundest seeing, the way of the Eternal. He will "render to Caesar the things that are Caesar's, and to God the things that are God's." In a time of spiritual disorder it is his special task to cherish the individual soul as the supreme gift of being, to bear witness to his vision of life in all its diversities and wholeness. He cannot be commanded in the name of social welfare and progress. His choice must remain a personal choice, made in conscience and in freedom, out of his love for the whole of God's creation.

"Dark midnight looms above the road, and leans over the highway with its stars. I cannot cross the road without treading upon the universe." Thus Pasternak and the voice of Tyutchev speaks to him out of the past, and makes his heart glad:

> Blessed the man who has his life
> In a time of change and destiny,
> Whom the exalted gods have called
> Unto their feast and company.
> A witness of celestial councils,
> He will behold their majesty,
> And, godlike, in his lifetime share
> Their cup of immortality.

Sewanee
Tennessee   EUGENE M. KAYDEN

Contents

MY SISTER LIFE

Summer of 1917

To Lermontov

About My Verses

Along the pavement I will grind
A dust half sun, half glass. My deeds
In winter time the ceiling hears;
My verse the cold damp corner reads.

To window frames my garret room
Will bow, rehearsing verse, and prove
How folly, trouble, and adventure
Can, bursting, leapfrog to the roof.

The storms will rage for endless days
And waste my means and ends estranged;
I'll suddenly remember suns
And find the world is long since changed.

Then Christmas like a crow will stare;
The boisterous day will playfully
Converse of matters unfamiliar
To my beloved and to me.

In a muffler, screwing up my eyes,
I'll fling the frosted window wide
And call into the court-yard: "Children!
What century have we outside?

Who cleared a pathway to my door,
That hole all choked with sleet and snow,
While I was smoking with Lord Byron,
Drinking with Edgar Allan Poe?"

Though long familiar, like Daryál,
I felt with Lermontov his truth—
The poet's hell, the poet's horror,
And soaked my life in his vermouth.

My Sister Life

My Sister Life's in flood, and breaks out
In the world about with showers of spring;
But jeweled folk are prideful and snappish;
Politely, like snakes in the grass, they sting.

The grown-ups, of course, have special reasons.
Your own, no doubt, are as foolish, I'd say:
That eyes and lawns in a storm are lilac,
That horizons smell like damp reseda.

In May, in the railway compartment, you study
The schedule of trains on a rural track;
They seem more important than holy scriptures
Or that the coaches are dusty and black.

The barking of brakes wakes up at each stop
Those villagers dulled by their homemade wines,
Who stare from their bunks: Is this my station?
The sun smiles at me before it declines.

The third signal bell swims splashing off
With sincere regrets: Your station is far!
In the miles of night, downgrade, the fields
Disappear between platform steps and a star.

Folk sleep in their houses, blinking; at home
My darling blissfully slumbers. The train
Sweeps on; while I dash along the platforms,
Each carriage door strews my heart on the plain.

[4]

The Weeping Garden

The garden is frightful! It drips, it listens:
  Is the rain in loneliness here,
Squeezing a branch like lace at a window,
  Or is there a witness near?

The earth is heavy with swollen burdens;
  Smothered, the spongy weald.
Listen! Afar, as though it were August,
  Night ripens in a field.

No sound. Not a stranger around to spy
  The night. In the garden alone,
Rain starts up again, dripping and tumbling
  On roof, gutter, flagstone.

I'll bring the rain to my lips, and listen:
  Am I in loneliness here,
In the rain, bursting with tears, in darkness,
  Or is there a witness near?

Deep silence. Not even a leaf is astir.
  No gleam of light to be seen.
Only choking sobs and the splash of his slippers,
  And his sighs and tears between.

In the Breeze

In the breeze that asks the branches
If it's time for birds to sing,
Like a sparrow wet with raindrops,
O my lilac bloom, you swing!

The rain drips heavy buttons.
The garden, gleaming, peers
Bespattered and besprinkled,
Blue with a million tears.

My sorrow nursed the garden
All in thorns because of you;
Last night it lived in fragrance
And murmured sweet in dew.

It shook the panes and shutters
Nightlong in fretfulness;
And a sudden bitter dampness
Passed lightly over your dress.

And roused by wondrous tidings
Of time and memories,
Today the morning gazes
With eyes like anemones.

Out of Superstition

A box of small red oranges—
   My narrow room.
And oh the grime of lodging rooms
   This side the tomb!

This cubbyhole, out of superstition,
   I chose once more.
The walls seem dappled oaks; the door,
   A singing door.

You strove to leave; my hand was steady
   Upon the latch.
My forelock touched a wondrous forehead;
   My lips felt violets.

O Sweet! Your dress as on a day
   Not long ago
To April, like a snowdrop, chirps
   A gay "Hello!"

I know your vestal air. You came
   With a chair today,
Took down my life as from a shelf,
   And blew the dust away.

"Fresh Paint"

"Fresh paint." I should have read the sign.
   The Soul all fear defies,
And memory's stained with calves and cheeks,
   And hands and lips and eyes.

But more than all good luck and sorrow
   You were to me most dear,
For whiter than white the yellowed world
   You made when you came near.

I know, O dearest, my own gloom
   Will whiter be somehow,
Than fever whiter, than the lampshade,
   Or the bandage round my brow.

Swaying on a Bough

Swaying on a bough sweet-scented,
And drinking this blissfulness warm
In the dark, from chalice to chalice
A raindrop fell dazed by the storm.

And gliding from chalice to chalice,
It slid along two—a great tear
It hung in each flower; an agate
It sparkled with trembling and fear.

The wind in the meadow blowing
May torture and flatten that drop,
But the pair will never be parted,
Or their kissing and drinking stop.

They sway and they laugh, each trying
To be free, again to depart,
But the stamens hug them so tightly
That a knife won't cut them apart.

Resting Oars

The boat sways in my drowsy breast;
Low willows lick my collarbone,
My elbows, oarlocks.—O let us rest!
It may happen like that to anyone.

It is the bliss we hear in bars
Of song. A lilac's hint of blue,
A glimpse of daisy heads in dew,
And lips to barter for the stars!

It means—embrace the boundless skies,
Fold in your arms great Heracles!
It means—for centuries at ease
Spend nights with nightingales and sighs!

Spring Rainstorm

The rain smiled at a wildcherry; drenched
The lacquer of cabs, the tremor of trees.
In moonlight, pop-eyed, the fiddlers filed
To the theatre.—Citizens, close your ranks!

Winds, pools of rain. As a throat choked
With tears, the innermost heart of roses
With jewels aflame! Rain, spout new joy
On roses, brows, eyelashes, clouds!

The moon silvers fluttering dresses,
Linked arms, the triumph of ravished lips,
And shapes in plaster their epic, shapes
A bust no hand has shaped in life.

Whose blood, in passion, suddenly flooded
The heart to the brim with hope and glory?
Behold, a leader's hand has gripped
Lips and aortas tight in its steel.

Not rain nor night nor multitudes striving
Together, shouting hurrahs to Kerensky,
But a blinding escape from catacombs
And last despairs, to the open, the light.

No roses, lips, or the roar of throats,
No rage of crowds in blind commotion,
But the swelling tides of Europe's unrest
In a storm exultant on asphalt squares.

An English Lesson

When Desdemona came a-singing,
And a little time to live had she—
Not love, her fatal star, she sobbed:
It was a willow, willow tree.

When Desdemona came a-singing,
With firmer voice and lifted head,
Her demon at her death prepared
A psalm of a weeping river bed.

And when Ophelia came a-singing,
And a little time to live had she—
Like storms that sweep a hayloft clean
Her soul from suffering was free.

And when Ophelia came a-singing,
With wild and bitter dreams to pine,
What trophies in her grave had she?
An armful of willow and celandine.

Their passions fell away like rags,
And silent into the pool of night
And time they went, with aching hearts,
Their loving forms transfused in light.

Definition of Poetry

It's a summons sternly swelling,
The cracking of shattered icefields,
The night that blasts young leaves,
The contest of two nightingales,

The stifled sweet pea on the vine,
The cry of a world at birth,
Figaro from flutes and the platform
In a crashing fall among rose beds.

It's all that night will reveal
In the depths of bathing places—
To carry a star to the garden
Alone in its trembling wet arms.

Like dank wood, the stifled mind,
When the sky is choked by alders;
Gay stars could rock with laughter
At blockheads sunk flat in mud.

Definition of the Soul

To fall off, a ripe pear in a storm,
With one leaf in loyalty bound.
O blind faith! To abandon the branch,
To choke in dry dust on the ground!

To fall, more aslant than the wind.
O blind faith: "I'm safe!" In a flash
Of glory it died in the storm,
And darkly it crumbled in ash.

My country's a blaze in the storm.
Say, fledgling, where now is your nest?
O my leaf, like a goldfinch in fear!
Why struggle, O shyest and best?

And whither, in fear, do you strive,
O my song, in parting from me?
Ah, the mortal "stay here" we despised
When together we throbbed on the tree.

Definition of Creative Art

With shirt wide open at the collar,
Maned as Beethoven's bust, it stands;
Our conscience, dreams, the night and love,
Are as chessmen covered by its hands.

And one black king upon the board:
In sadness and in rage, forthright
It brings the day of doom.—Against
The pawn it brings the mounted knight.

In gardens where from icy spheres
The stars lean down and linger near,
Tristan still sings like a nightingale
On Isolde's vine, with trembling fear.

The gardens, ponds, and fences, made pure
By burning tears, and the whole great span,
Creation—are only forms of passion
Hoarded in the heart of man.

Sparrow Hills

My kisses across your breast, like water from a jug!
They'll have an end, and soon, our days of summer heat.
Nor shall we every night raise up in trailing dust
The hurdy-gurdy's bellow, stamp and drag our feet.

I've heard about old age. What ominous forebodings!
That no wave will lift again to the stars its hands,
That waters will speak no more; no god in the woods;
No heart within the pools; no life in meadowlands.

O rouse your soul! This frenzied day is yours to have!
It is the world's midday. Why don't you use your eyes?
Behold, there's thought upon high hills in seething bubbles
Of heat, woodpeckers, cones and needles, clouds and skies.

Here tracks of city trolleys stop, and further
The pines alone must satisfy. Trams cannot pass.
It is always Sunday there! Plucking little branches,
There the clearing capers, slipping on the grass.

And strewing sunrays, Whitsun, and rambling walks,
The woods will have us say the world was always so:
Conceived like that by forests, hinted to the meadows,
And spilt by clouds upon us as though on chintz below.

Mein Liebchen, Was Willst Du Noch Mehr?

Arrow hands raced down the walls.
The hours are beetles in the grasses.
Stop, why hurl the plates about,
Sound the alarm, smash the glasses?

Even in this country cottage
Things can't shape themselves like that.
Who in love is lucky—always?
Do not fear the thunderclap!

It may strike, and flare like a wet
Cabin charged by lightning rings.
Then they'll give away the puppies.
Rain-blown shots will pierce their wings.

Let the forest be our hallway
Warm in moonlight. Life is fair!
Trouble's like a new-washed apron
Hung to dry in lisping air.

And if waterspouts of sadness
Drive you forth, the storms will roar,
Storms will praise your well-kept house:
Can you really ask for more?

As a gnat inside an oil lamp
So one year has burned away.
See, he got up wet and sleepy
In the grey-blue dawn of day.

See, he's peering through the window
Dread with pity, old with fears.
See, his pillow's wet with crying
Where he buried deep his tears.

What will please that ragged body?
Oh, who never smile on gladness,
What in the empty summer days
Will allay your stifling sadness?

Woods are veiled with leaden fringes,
And the burdock's sad and grey.
Let him weep. But you are lovely,
In your eagerness like day!

Why's that numskull crying? Can he
Feel the lovers' heart of trust?
Are, then, sunflowers in the village
Dimmed, like suns, by rain and dust?

Sultry Night

A drizzle fell. It did not bend
The grasses in the thunder's track.
Dust swallowed up the pills of raindrops
Like iron powdered soft and black.

The village hoped for no salvation,
And low the poppy, swooning, waved;
Inflamed, the standing rye grew red,
Defiled—a god that raved.

Throughout the orphaned, sleepless, vast,
Sick meadowlands in open spaces
The storms lay dying, still, and wails
Flew headlong from the dwelling places.

Close after them came blindly fleeing
A scant few drops. Beside the fence,
Between wet branches and the wind,
A quarrel rose. My heart grew tense.

They spoke of me. I felt the garden
Would chatter, fearful, long in heat.
But in the talk of bush and shutters
I went unnoticed from the street.

If they see me here, I can't go back:
They'll chatter, chatter, to the end.

A Still More Sultry Dawn

All morning long the pigeon cooed
At your window.
In water troughs
Like sleeves of dampened shirts
Lay branches, dying.
A drizzle fell. Small clouds
Came lightly through a dusty market place,
Lulling my sadness,
So I feared,
Upon a hawker's tray.
I prayed they'd stop in flight.
I thought they would.
Dawn came ashen, as the talk of prison mates,
As a squabble stirred among the bushes.

I prayed the hour would come
When behind your windows,
Your water-basin, like a mountain ice drift
Would roar
With scraps of broken song,
And cheek and forehead warm from sleep
Would glow as ice within a burning glass
Upon your dressing table.
But the spheres because of talk
Beneath the banner of the scudding clouds
Did not hear the prayer
I murmured in snow-powdered silence,
Drenched like an overcoat,
Like dusty sounds of busy threshing,
Like a loud squabble among the bushes.
I begged them:
Stop your torture,
Let me sleep!—
A mist rose up, and tramping,

The clouds passed through the dusty market
Like recruits plodding their way to fields.
They trudged in endless time,
Like captive Austrians,
Like silence moaning,
Ever moaning:
"Please, give us
Water!"

Moochkap

My heart is stifled; the horizon's like
My thoughts—dirt-brown, inferior
Tobacco. These windmills bring to mind
A seashore, grey sails, a sloop of war.

And why her late arrival, troubling
My sight with tubs, crab claws, spare sails,
With superfluous slime of tears veiling
The gleam of fishes' heads and scales?

And oh the hour slips, like a pebble
In shallows ricocheting, down
The bay. Not sinking, no! It's there
Like my thoughts—tobacco, faded brown.

Then shall I see her soon? One hour
Of waiting here before her train,
One hour gripped tight by apathy
Of hellish dark and storm again.

Summer 1917

Athirst, we longed in discontent
For moths and butterflies;
About us the woven memories
Of summer, mint, and honey.

No chime of clocks but ringing flails
From dawn to evening dusk,
Stinging the air with panting dreams
Enravished by the weather.

Sometimes the gladsome sunset, idling,
Surrendered to cicadas
And stars and trees its governance
Of kitchens and of gardens.

The moon spread long uneven beams
Or hid itself in dark;
And softly, softly flowed the night
From cloud to passing cloud.

Not like a shower, but in a dream,
In shy forgetfulness,
The rain was shuffling at the door,
With the smell of winecorks in the air.

The smell in dust, the smell in grass.
And if one cared to learn,
The smell of gentry copybooks
Was all of rights and brotherhood.

The councils met in the villages;
You, at their meetings, too?
The days hung bright like sorrel,
The smell of winecorks in the air.

Summer Thunderstorm

Then Summer said goodbye
To the station. Tipping its cap,
The thunder took as souvenirs
A hundred blinding snaps.

The lilac darkened. With armfuls
Of lightning, plucked in the night,
He flooded from the meadows
The overseer's house with light.

And when a wave of malice
The roof had overflowed,
And like charcoal on a drawing
Rains rushed in a solid flood,

The crumbling sense began to blink:
It seemed, though bright and gay,
The mind in its remotest corners
Would be lighted clear as day.

Darling, It Frightens Me!

Darling, it frightens me! A poet
In love loves like a pagan god.
Chaos then creeps to light again
As when the world was first begot.

His eyes weep tons of mist. Shrouded
In clouds, he seems of mammoth size.
He's out of date. Our times are new:
He's not in step; he's uncivilized!

He sees how people wed, get drunk,
Then sleep it off, and how the spawn
Of swampy frogs, by marriage rites,
Becomes the best caviar in town.

They squeeze the gift of life, this pearl
By a Watteau, into a narrow box.
They hate the man who shows them up
For the vain and coward weathercocks

They are. They cringe, they lie like drones.
They mock because from common clay
He lifts a woman up in her worth,
A bacchante from her amphora.

The dawn of day burns in his breath,
Andean peaks, by the sign and power
Of starry dust, while village nights
Reel, bleating, paler every hour.

Today the reek of ancient gullies,
Each murky fecund vestry-room,
Like a mattress-bed of typhoid pain,
Festers in its jungle gloom.

Postscript

No, I am not the cause of your sorrow.
It was not for me you left your country.
It was the sunlight aflame on drops of ink
As on clusters of dusty currants.

In the veins of my thoughts and letters
Cochineal appeared.
That purple was not of my making.
No, I am not the cause of your sorrow.

It was the evening, moulded of dust, when panting,
I kissed you, smothered by your ochre, pollen.
It was the shadows feeling your pulse.
By the fences you opened your face to the plains;
You flamed in the air and the varnish of gates
Flooded by twilight, poppy, and ash.

It was summertime glowing in labels
Alongside the pools, like bags in the heat of the sun,
That stamped the boatman's chest as with wax,
That scorched your dresses and hats.

It was your lashes closed from the sunshine;
It was the sun, untamed, that had polished its horns
On the fences, butting and smashing stockades.
It was the west in your hair like a ruby
That buzzed and slowly died
Into purple and raspberry red.
No, not I, but you—all your beauty I loved.

In Memory of THE DEMON

He came in the night
In blue glacier light, from Tamara.
His wings pointed out
Where nightmares hold sway, or fade.

He cried not, maligned not
The scourged, the naked, the bruised.
The gravestone still stands
By the fence near the Gruzian shrine.

Hunchbacked, grim,
The shadow sat resolute under the grating.
The guitar, by the lamp,
Was silent and shy about the princess.

Light sparkled in his hair;
It crackled like phosphor.
The colossus refused to hear
That the Caucasus grows older with sorrow.

Not far from the windows,
While plucking his woolen burnoose,
He swore by the snows:
Sleep, dearest! In an avalanche soon I return.

THEMES AND VARIATIONS

Encounter

Nightlong and through the early morning,
Since six o'clock, since four, since two,
Water rushed out of pipes and holes
And pools, off fences, wind, and roofs.

The walks grew slippery, the winds
Had ripped the water like gunny sack,
And one could go as far as Podolsk
And nowhere meet a soul abroad.

At six o'clock, in a break of landscape,
From a stairway sodden with the damp,
A weary "See you then tomorrow"
Split off and plunged into the water.

Somewhere with automatic pulleys
And rattling chains, anticipating
A day of water-drains, the East
Mechanically worked her spell.

Tricked out in frowzy finery,
Horizons drowsed above frosted kvass,
And coughed, and loudly shouted after
Their heady bouillabaisse of March.

The author and the March Night came
Together, still arguing, side by side,
Led homeward by the chilly landscape—
The pair led home from a meeting place.

The March Night and the author walked
In a hurry home, but spied from time
To time a phantom flashing past them,
Or vanishing before their eyes.

The dawn! As at an amphitheater,
When people heed the precursor's call,
The Tomorrow on the steps proclaimed
Rushed, fluttering, to meet the pair.

It came like a joiner with his frame:
Then houses, trees, and temples seemed
As lost, as alien in this world,
In the frame's unattainable expanse.

The pair soon spoke in hexameters.
They changed, slipped to the right across
That frame. But trimmers were dragged off
For dead, and no one marked their loss.
   1922

Mephistopheles

On Sundays from beyond the turnpike
And piled-up dust, they trooped pellmell,
While showers, finding them away
From home, burst in their bedroom windows.

At dinner time it was their custom
To serve some scanty shares of rain,
While the whirlwind darted on its wheel
Around the cupboards in the room.

And while the silken window blinds
At home rolled straightway to the ceiling,
The ponds, the flowers, the open air
Tugged hard at all the dolts and oafs.

Later long lines of carriages
Drew together around the city wall
Where a shadow, scaring all the horses,
Every night came suddenly alive.

In blood-red stockings held by ribbons
His fiendish legs, like tracking straps
Hung from a drum, kicked up the dust
On highways drenched in sunset rays.

It seemed that, whirled up in a stream
Of arrogance from overhanging leaves,
The sun's disdain would level worlds,
But put up only with these feathers.

He looked on folk as only signposts,
And scarcely touched his hat in greeting;
He strode on, shaking loud with laughter,
And, merry, hugged his friend alone.

Shakespeare

A coaching yard, and, looming over the river
In terraces, the gloomy Tower set back.
The clanking of hoofs and the rheumy pealing
Of Westminster, from muffled piles in black.

The narrow streets. The reeking houses, crowded,
That hoard the damp in their branching timbers,
Morose from soot and sodden from ale;
And crooked lanes by London fogs enshrouded.

The snow falls sluggishly in darkness.
It came tumbling at twilight, wrinkled somewhat,
Half drowsy, like a crumpling belly band,
And smothered each deserted sleepy lot.

A small window, with bits of violet mica
In leaden rims. . . . "Damn this weather!
We may sleep in the cold, in the open yet.
Now on to a barrel! Hey, barber, water!"

As he shaves, he cackles, holding his sides
At the wit of a jester jabbering since dinner
And straining through a pipe stuck to his lips
His tedious trifles.
                But Shakespeare bides,
Impatient with jesting and bored by the saws.
The sonnet he wrote with not one blot,
At white heat, last night at that far table
Where curdled rennet laps at lobster claws—
The sonnet speaks to him:
                     "Sir, I acclaim
Your talents, but, O my poet and master,
Do you know—you and that dolt astride
That barrel there with soap on his mug,

I'm swifter than lightning, nobler by nature
Than mortals? In brief, that, scourged in my flame,
You begin to stink like your foul tobacco?

"Forgive me, old man, my filial skepticism,
But, Sir, my good lord, I believe we lie
At an inn. Are your cronies my kind? Your verse,
For the mob? Sir, grant me the infinite sky!

"Well, read it to him! Why not? In the name
Of all guilds and bills—in his company—
Five yards away—at billiards with him,
Do you like this sort of popularity?"

"Read to him? Are you mad?" He calls for the waiter.
And fiddling with a bunch of Malaga grapes,
He reckons: half pint, French stew. And he runs,
Flinging his napkin at the phantom shape.

   1919

The Racing Stars

The racing stars. Headlands washed in wash of seas.
The salt spray blinded. And tears grew dry.
Night filled the bedrooms. The racing thoughts.
The Sphinx in stillness watched the Sahara sky.

The candles flared. It seemed the blood froze
In the huge Colossus. Lips smiled inside
The swelling blue smile of the wilderness.
Night faded with the ebbing of the tide.

A breeze from far Morocco stirred the sea.
The simoom blew. Arkhángelsk snored in snows.
The candles flared. The first draft of *The Prophet*
Lay dry. And morning on the Ganges rose.
   1918

That May Happen
(from MALADY: 3)

That may happen one way or another,
At a certain fateful hour
When, gagging you, blacker than monks and clergy
Insanity may get you down.

Frost. The night outside the window watches,
As is its custom, the firming ice.
Inside its fur coat, sunk in that armchair,
The Soul is purring on and on the same old tune.

Its cheek, the profile of a bough,
The poker's shadow, and the parquet floor,
Mould out of remorse and dreaming
The guilty blizzard raging long for days.

The night is still. The night is clear and frosty.
Like a blind puppy lapping milk
The palings drink the starlight among
Fir trees deep in unfathomable gloom.

Perhaps the fir trees gleam, perhaps they drip,
Perhaps a taper's flaring in the night.
The snow blinds fir after fir beneath its paws,
The trees are silhouetted against other trees.

Perhaps the silence, perhaps the sky,
Or the elegy of telegraphic waves,
Was a longing for the cry of "Answer!"
Or was it the echo of another silence?

Perhaps no hearing lives in twigs and needles,
No hearing in the silence of the spheres;
Perhaps the gleam's the answer down ethereal ranges
To someone's lingering "Hullo!"

Frost. The night outside the window watches,
As is its custom, the firming ice.
Inside its fur coat, sunk in that armchair,
The Soul is purring on and on the same old tune.

Oh, his lips! He bites them till they bleed.
He's trembling; his face is in his hands.
For his biographer that chalklike face
And gestures portend a storm of speculation.

January 1919

That year! How often by the window
The old year muttered, tempting me, "Jump out!"
But with a Christmas tale of Dickens
The new year puts despondency to rout.

He whispers: "Shake it off." He checks
The thermometer, the rising sun outside.
The old year talked to me of strychnine,
And fell into a vial of cyanide.

Our peace he scoops up with his dawn,
His hands, his wildly streaming locks of hair—
Our peace from roofs and birds outside,
A peace unknown to old philosophers.

He came, he stretched himself in light
From panels, himself in service to the snow.
He's insolent, beside himself;
He shouts, he calls for drinks, he makes a show,

He's wild and rowdy! He brings with him
The vulgar street! What can we do?—Be sure,
There's not a grief in all the world
So great the snows of winter will not cure.

Entwine This Shower
(from SEPARATION, 5)

Entwine this shower, like a wave, cool elbows,
Like lilies all satin and strong, with languid hands!
To the fields! Rejoice! Lay hold! In this boisterous race
The woods are resounding with echoes of hunts in Calydon,
Where Actaeon rashly pursued Atalanta, like a roe;
Where they kissed in the glade, in infinite azure
That whistled by the ears of the horses;
Where they kissed in the passionate baying of the chase,
In the pealing of horns, and the cracking of trees,
And the noise of hoofs and claws.
To the fields! To the fields! even like those.

   1918

The Trembling Piano
(*from SEPARATION, 9*)

The trembling piano will lick the foam from its lips.
This frenzy will undo your heart. "Dearest,"
You whisper. "No!" I shout back to you. "Never!
While playing music?"—And yet we are nearest

In twilight here, the music tossed upon
The fire, year after year, like pages of a diary.
O wondrous obit and memories that ever beckon,
And strike the spirit dumb! Look, you are free!

I do not hold you. Go. Do good to others.
Go from me. *Werther* can't be written again.
But in our time the air's defiled with death:
To open a window is like opening a vein.
   1918

Thus Life Begins

Thus life begins: When two years old,
They live in light and melody;
They chirp, they babble. Then the gold
Of words they find when they are three.

And thus they learn to understand.
But in the din of turbines whirled
About, their own seem not their own,
Their humble home a foreign world.

What trouble broods that menacing
Wild beauty—there by the lilac tree—
If to steal children's not the thing?
Thus fear will breed anxiety

And greater fears. Can one endure
A star, who feels one's bound to win,
Like Faust, although a dreamer pure
And simple? Thus gypsy ways begin.

Then soaring over roofs and fences,
Where cottage folk should feel at home,
They descry unlooked for seas afar.
So first iambic verses come.

Thus summer nights will, kneeling, pray
In wheaten fields *Thy will be done*,
Yet strive against the light of Day,
And pick a quarrel with the Sun.

Thus poetry sets them on their way.
1921

We Are Few

We are few. Perhaps three: a dark
Infernal lot, embittered, wet
Beneath a grey and racing bark
Of rains, low clouds—the soviet
Of soldiers, of debates and curses,
Disputes about fares and verses.

We used to be men. An epoch now.
We are swept on caravan trails
As the tundra's swept in the sough
Of pistons, tender, and rails.
We swoop, break through, interpose,
And are off, a whirlwind of crows.

You'll not understand until late.
When winds in the morning confound
The thatch of the roofs, a debate
In the congress of trees will resound,
Astir with immortal speech
Where the shingled roofs do not reach.

   1921

My Pictures Swing

My pictures swing in the thundershower
With a wind that blows my candles out,
But I cannot stop their swinging rhyme
And measure on walls and hooks about.

Suppose the world is behind a mask,
Against the mind's free play? Suppose,
That some will dare to cement its mouth,
And seal it against the winter snows?

And yet all masks fly off in time,
Despite convention, honor, power,
If there is good reason for a song,
If there is the season for a shower.

1922

In the Wood

The wood is clouded with cathedral darkness,
And heavy with lilac heat the meadow glares.
What's left to them—for secrecy and kissing?
Like wax in eager hands, the world is theirs.

Such is the changeless dream: You do not sleep,
But dream you long for sleep, that someone lies
In dreaming near, that underneath his eyelids
Two suns sear black the lashes of his eyes.

The sunlight ebbs. The iridescent beetles.
The glass of dragonflies and wings ablaze
Across their cheeks. The woodland gleams like gems
In a watchmaker's hands, alert with sunset rays.

It seems he slumbers to the tick of numbers,
While in the amber sky the spirits place
A regulated clock within the ether
As if to gauge the change of heat in space.

They shift it round about, shake needles down,
Strew shadows, nettles; they swing and bore into
The day's fatigue a swelling mast of shadows
Upon the clock-face shimmering in blue.

It seems their bliss is old, like fallen leaves,
And that the woodland holds their sunset dreams.
But happy couples do not watch the clock;
They sleep, as these two lovers—so it seems.

1917

The House at Spásskoye

This memorable September's strewn about Spásskoye.
Is today the time for your leaving the villa?
Beyond fences the Echo replied to the herdsman,
Rang out in the woods to the stroke of the axe.

The marshes shivered near the park last night.
As soon as the sun reappeared, it went down.
No harebell will drink of rheumatic dews;
Now the lilac dropsy has smutted the birches.

Disconsolate woods. They are longing for rest
Under snows, the unwaking slumber of bear dens.
The trees among stumps, inside blackened fences,
Gape like an obituary in a black border.

More faded and spotted the birchwood each day,
Still thinner and duller its aqueous shade. . . .
He's grumbling: You are fifteen years old again,
But what, O my child, can we do with them now?

There are many, I'd say—not a matter for jesting—
Like mushrooms by hedges, like birds in a bush.
We've shrouded too often our own horizon,
And veiled new views of life with their mists.

On his deathbed the typhus-feverish clown
Hears the gallery's roar of Homeric laughter.
The same agony beholds, in hallucination,
From the highway now this timbered old house.
   1918

So Be It

The dawn swings wild the candlelight,
And strikes the martin with its flame.
I search my memory and say:
Let life be always new again!

The dawn is like a rifleshot
Upon the night. A hissing flame
In air, slow dying in its flight.
Let life be always new again!

The breeze is at the door, the same
That huddled, trembling, near our house
At night, and shivered in the rain.
Let life be always new again!

That fellow's singularly odd.
Why does he barge into the guard?
The sign is plain: "No thoroughfare."
Let life be always new again!

Then wave the traffic flag in air,
And play the master of a day,
As long as men this darkness walk,
And while the country is in flames.
   1919

I've Come from the Street

I've come from the street, O Spring! There poplars stand
Amazed, horizons tremble, houses fear they may fall!
There the air is blue like the bundle of linen
A patient takes home, on leaving the hospital.

There the evening's blank, like a story begun
By a star, but broken off without a conclusion,
While a thousand riotous eyes stare empty of mind
And thought, in immeasurable deep confusion.
   1918

Spring

The air is scourged by driving rains;
The ice, a scabby grey. And you gaze
The harder for the sky to waken;
It wakes with wind and storm ablaze.

As always, with overcoat unbuttoned,
With muffler open at the chest,
He'll drive the screeching birds ahead,
The frenzied birds at every nest.

He's sure to see you, and, untidy,
He'll scrape the candle drippings, squint
And yawn, and say it's safe to take
The cover from your hyacinth.

As always, senseless, in confusion,
He'll ruffle his hair-mop, stammering,
To stun you with scurvy, stupid tales
Of me—my coming in the spring.
   1918

Poetry

Poetry, I swear an oath to you,
I'll swear until I'm hoarse with pain!
You're not a stiff-shirt, prim sweet singer;
You're summer townsfolk come third-class;
You're suburbs, not a vain refrain.

You're hot like summer city streets,
And tougher than a camp at night,
Where clouds, oppressive, groaning, pass,
Or scamper quickly out of sight.

By curving rails divided, you are
No stale old tune, but suburbs dear
To me where men come home from work
Not gay with song but still with fear.

The sprouts of rain, in grapevines mired,
In the long, long night till dawn will pine,
And scrawl from dripping roofs acrostics,
With bubbles in the rhyming line.

When undoubted truths, O Poetry,
Are held like buckets at the tap,
The hoarded stream will spout—for me
In my open copybook to trap.

   1922

Enigma's Fingernail Mark

Here the trail of enigma's fingernail mark:
"Let me rest for the night; at dawn I'll read
It again, to be clear. Till I wake, no being
Can move the beloved as I when I plead."

You thrilled to the brass of my lips even so,
As an audience is moved by actors in form.
My kiss was like summer, a lingering kiss,
That gradually burst into storm.

I drank like the birds. I sucked till I swooned.
In my gullet the stars, their starry delight.
Thus nightingales, quivering, roll their eyes,
As they drain drop by drop the starry night.
   1918

TWO REVOLUTIONS

Bloody Sunday
(from THE YEAR 1905)

Night. Petersburg.
The air swells dark with icy flakes
under needling footsteps;
no street's forbidden
to fur coats and those in sheepskins.
The moon shrinks smaller by half in the frost.
The Neva district stirs.
Crowds clear a way:
There! Gapon!

The hall rings loud
in airless heat.
Five thousand in the press.
From the street the blown snow
clings to stairways in the hall.
Here's the new nativity:
against the walls
of a dingy vaulted womb
pulses
a strange unlovely lump—
our newborn age.

The dawn of glory.
Clouds in black and cranberry hues.
Halls and passages creak,
and slops steam in the streets.
On the run they come to the gates
from meeting places
to follow
sacred banners
in the open cold,
in the blaze
of winter day.

Eight roaring waves
and then the ninth,
majestic as space.
Caps off, they chant as they go,
Save Thy people, O Lord!
Canal and bridge to left;
to right, the graveyard gates;
at rear, soundless trees,
and telegraph wires in front.

Pavements rise on stilts
on Kamennoi Island;
crowds stare from curbs and doorways.
Behind the slow procession
long trails
of crowded streets and lanes.
They near the Palace Park.
They march over Trinity Bridge.

Eight volleys from the Neva
and then the ninth,
as weary as glory.
Ho, they scud to right and left!
Ho, spaces thunder forth:
Beware, we'll get even with you!
This is the hour of rending
at the joints
of loyalty sworn
to rulers.

Fugitive sidewalks,
deeper dusk,
and the fallen dead.
On barricades volleys answer

to the cannonade's roar.
I'm fourteen years,
and in a month—fifteen.
These days are my diary
to be read at will
at any page.

We play a game of snowflakes.
We catch them spinning
out of the sky—
flakes of hearsay and talk of the times.
This landslide.of kingdoms
in the high-school yard,
and the reeling of snows
in January.

Stormwinds day after day.
The lads who are in the Party
look like eagles
and act grown up.
The smaller boys
are rude with their tutors,
push desks to the walls,
play at parliament in class,
and daydream
about forbidden slums of the poor.

For three days running
it snows,
then clears up at night.

Next morning
we hear the shattering news:
Our high-school patron,
Sergei Alexandrich,
bombed
in the Kremlin. . . .
In those first days in February
I grew up to love the mighty storm.

   1925

Mutiny at Sea
(from THE YEAR 1905)

In time all matters pall.
You never have a chance.
In the welter of days
and of years and ages,
in the white rage
of waves,
in the white trance
of acacias,
only the sea, to be sure,
alone the sea
cuts you down to size.

Your throne, O Sea,
on mounds of nets.
Your shout rings loud in the skies;
you're gay as spring
in play
when breezes wave a fugitive lock
around a sailor's brow
on watch at the prow.
You please the children playful in spray.
Or tossing, you trumpet in storms
when the elements battle
and call you home.

Then the ancient of time
and chaos
in spume of seas,
hoarse with ravenous waves,
dashes with hatred
satanic,
a monster roaring with ruin and graves,
and, livid with ooze,
it crumbles the stones at the port.

Sails in their fear of darkness
huddle beneath the walls
of storm and rains.
Skies crouch lower
flying downward
steep
sea slopes
and finger the deep
with wings of clamorous gulls.

Weary they come
gasping,
electric with storm and dark
in infernal chaos of clouds;
rocking,
laboring slow,
they heave into port.
Blue-limbed lightnings
leap like toads into pools.
Forerigging and shrouds
shattered—
topsail yard to deck.

Ready for slumber at last.
With evening crabs
stirring for shelter,
and aster heads nodding
in the wearisome sun,
the sea, rippling,
purrs.
The grey-flushed hulk
of a steel-clad battleship
rust-speckled
heaves in the ebb.

Sundown.
The warship *Potémkin*
flamed in sight
electric with light.
From spardeck to mouldy caboose,
invaded by myriads of galley-flies,
tainted stew meat
they served the crew. . . .
Darkness embroiled the sea.
The portholes pitted the darkness;
lights brooded till daybreak,
then shuddered, and died.

Great mounds of morning surges
glided
like mercurial razors
away from the shining hulk.
Towering above them
the battleship waked to the sound of a bell
for morning prayers.
Men shuffled to swab every deck.
At dinner they sulked
in revolt at pots and kettles.
They gulped dry bread and water,
they chewed hardtack in silence.
Then a voice yelled out:
"All hands on deck!
On watch! To your places!"
Someone in white
purple with gall
cursed,
bellowed:
"Attention!"

"Not satisfied, eh?
Back to the kettles!
If not, to the yards! Step quick!"
The watch looked dazed.
Sudden, with one impulse, together
they rushed in riot
to the guns.
"Hold back!"
shouted in rage their master and lord.

Some paused in their tracks.
He blocked their escape.
"A plot? Mutiny?"
He yelled a command:
"Ensign! tarpaulin! the haul!
Sentries, the chains!"
Other poor wretches
huddled in the maws of gun towers,
and waited in terror the lash and chains.

Sailor hearts
throbbed in fear.
One boy could stand it no longer,
and in agony shouted:
"Mates! Come on!
Kill them!
To the guns! For liberty!
Fight!"
Men leaped from the turrets
to the decks
for the fight.

And the mutiny winged
like a flame
from mizzen to bridge.
It spurted,
it crackled,
it spanned the air like an arc.
"Why run, mates?
Look out,
we'll get even with you!"
Trac-tac-tac! . . .
They picked them off
on the run.

Trac-tac-tac! . . .
Bullets spattered the decks,
or they found their prey
on the waves.
They crackled in air
in broadsides of fire
at their heels,
trac-tac-tac!
Overboard with them!
They jeered:
"Get out to your Navy review!"

Down by the turbines,
hot and eager,
men waited for news,
when, like a stoker's shadow,
towering tall,
Matushénko
peered
into the pits below,
and shouted:
"Okay, Steve! We got 'em!"

Steve clambered up,
and grinning, embraced him.
"We'll do without 'em, don't worry!
A few under guard;
for the rest, the sea.
How's the junior engineer?"
"With us, to be sure."
"Good! Send him to me,
on the bridge."

Day came to a close.
At sunset,
curtained by smoke,
through the tube
a sailor boomed to sailors below:
Anchors! Aweigh!
The voice grew still in the clouds.
The battleship sailed for Odessa,
forging furrows of doom,
rust-speckled,
aglow.
   1926

A *Testament*
(*from* LIEUTENANT SCHMIDT')

"In vain in days of chaos
We look for a happy end:
Some bear their Golgotha;
Some judge, and some repent.

"Like you, I am an atom
In a time of transformation,
And I accept your verdict—
Resigned, without vexation.

"I'm sure you have the power
To sweep me off your stage,
O martyrs of your dogma,
O victims of your age!

"For thirty years I've cherished
My country's destiny,
Yet I do not ask or hope for
Your magnanimity.

"The days we brood upon,
Remembering their roar,
Were days of surging waves
That hurled me to the fore.

"It was hard to stand aloof,
And harder not to give
My life. I don't regret
The way I chose to live.

"I stand between two eras
At war, and I rejoice:
The post between two camps
I occupy by choice."
    1927

Sublime Malady

I

The moving riddle gleams, and still
The siege goes on, day after day,
For months, with passing of the years.
One winter day the weary pickets
Come shouting, breathless, with the news:
The stronghold has surrendered!
We doubt, believe; estates in flames;
The vaulted rooms are blown to dust.
We search for doors, go in and out,
While days and months and years flit by.
The shadows deepen with the years.
The tale of Troy is born again.
We doubt, believe; estates in flames.
Impatient, some expect the army.
We're weak and blind. Day after day
High prison walls are blown to dust.

I am ashamed, each day ashamed,
That in an age of shadows
Our sublime old malady of thought
Still calls itself a song.
Are alleys, shrill in their upheaval,
Our song of toil and soil—
Our song from books and ages hurled
Against steel bayonets?
But hell is paved with good intentions.
It is our modern view
That if verses too are paved with them
Our sins will be forgiven.
Small talk must wound the ears of silence
Back from the fields of war;
How keen the ears of silence are
The days of desolation know.

In those swift-passing days we had
A lust for rumors. The winter nights
Bred lice and fears unweariedly,
As horses prick up their ears in fear.
The ears of silent darkness stirred
For days, ears choked with snow;
We became as fairy tales at night
On restless pillows sweet with mint.

By spring a fear came down upon
Upholstered stalls in concert halls.
Each day turned dingier with slush.
They gurgled, spewed their blood
And muttered secrets in the ears
Of waiting rooms, perhaps of this
And that small chat, of railway fares,
Of soldiers from the front on foot,
The thaw, or anything at all.
One goes to sleep—to wait for death,
But talkers turn up with taller tales.
In slush galoshes come and go;
The lice in mufflers and fur coats
Confound half-truths with lies, and prick
Their ears for sad unending days.

Although the thistle of every dawn
That strove to make its shadows longer
Could scarce by striving hard stretch out
The hours of day; although, as of old,
The boggy road dragged every wheel
Through sands up to the sloping top
Again, to bear it to safer ground
By way of sounder village stakes;
Although the vault of autumn skies
Grew dark, the forests far away,

The evenings cold with damp and haze—
We fooled ourselves!
The easeful slumber of the earth
Was in fact an unforeseen convulsion,
A death, a silence of the graves,
Resembling a peculiar stillness
Which shrouds the countryside in sleep
But shudders every now and then
In a vain struggle to remember:
What was it, please, I've tried to say?

Although the ceiling, as before,
In shoring up a chamber-room,
Pulled up the second to the third,
And then the fifth floor to the sixth,
Thus hinting by a show of floors
All's well as ever in the world—
We fooled ourselves!
The climbing waterpipes, I tell you,
Sucked up shrill cries of evil days.
The stench of laurel and chop suey
Cooked in the smoke of newspapers
Defiled for a mile the stale, dull air,
And grumbled: Why, a moment, please,
What did they have to eat today?

And creeping like a hungry tapeworm
From the second floor to the third,
And from the fifth floor to the sixth,
The stench advanced with filth and sloth
To slay the voice of loving-kindness.
What shall we ever do? Our cries
Had vanished in the clanging air,
And, falling on the railway station,

Their tumult passed the water tower
And disappeared beyond the groves
Where the embankments flared like gashes,
Where snowdrifts driven to and fro
Lay piled up high among the pines,
Where iron rails grew blind with itching
By contact with the rising storms.

Behind it all, in a glow of legends,
The intellectual, the hero, came,
The fool inflamed by his decrees
And drivel blared abroad in praise
Of evil forces that mocked him now
From every corner with a grin,
Because of his exploits, his stark
Belief that two twice two will make
An hundred in a trice—perhaps.
Behind it all, in a glow of legends,
The intellectual-idealist
Blazoned in print his happiness
About the sunset of his age.

Then knaves in furs began to face
Our ancient past, our North of darkness,
While the snows still busily contended
With death in the murk of endless night.
Like an organ, there upon the ice
Of mirrors the railway station flashed
In secret, staring open-eyed,
Telling about its wretched state
And emptiness, about repairs
And holidays, while striving hard
To keep its looks a little longer.
The intolerable frightful typhus,

Clasping us quietly by the knees,
Mused long and moveless, shuddering,
To hear the running tunes about
The crumbling palaces in dust.
Then from the hollow organ rose,
Like dust within the seams of bellows,
The weary strains of slow decay.
Its faithful and exacting ear
Continued to entreat the mist,
The ice, and pools along the floors,
To keep if possible their silence.

We were this music of the ice:
I speak of my own society
With which I now intend to leave
The stage, as I for one must leave.
There is no room for shame:
I wasn't made to look three times,
Afraid, three sundry ways at men;
Yet more absurd than any song
Our word "the enemy."
I'm grieved to find in each far land
This malady of mind.
All my life I've longed to be like others,
But the world's great age
Is stronger than my private yearning
And wants to be—like me.

We were the music of the teacups
Come round for tea and cake in shade
Of voiceless trees, in secret ways
Unworthy of the mind of man.
In winter cold the rooks wheeled high
In stiller skies, but our frosty year,

Ashamed, stood waiting at the gates.
We were the music of pure thought,
Barren in works; come winter time,
Our indecision turned to ice
The servants' yard and kitchen stairs.
But, hear me! I myself observed
The great Ninth Congress of Soviets.
I ran for hours in slush, I cursed
The streets, I cursed my luck, before
I got there on the second day,
Excited, to see the deputies,
And proud to show my official pass.

In sober mood, by sober roads
I came. Around me lay a city
In ruins, ravaged, and unreal,
Refusing flatly—so it seemed—
To rise, get going, to rebuild
Her walls again. . . .
Now snow-clad trees began to dream
Their spring, not for themselves alone,
But for a commonwealth of good
Through generations. And on that day
The story of the Congress seemed
A lesson on a magic canvas—
That the fever of our noblest minds
Is whiter, stronger than cement
If suddenly, week after week,
The builders in their pride behold
The rising walls of cities, ports,
And factories. . . .
We know, on a saner view we know,
We've left behind our witless talk,
The commonplace, the trite set speeches,

That time wiped out our winter ills
And quarrels of the past. . . .
Awake, O Poet! Show your pass!
No dozing, comrade, in this meeting! . . .
How shall I end my story now?

II

I still remember his living voice
That pierced me with encircling flames
Like jagged lightning at the neck.
We rose up with a shout, our eyes
Ransacking thoroughly the platform,
When suddenly he grew—grew taller
Even before he came on the stage.
He entered, unobserved, through lanes
Of crowded doors and helping hands,
As a ball of lightning in a storm
Flames bright and blinding in a room.

The thunder of wild applause rang out
To our relief, like a discharge
Of bursting cannonballs, beyond
Control, uncurled, through rings of space.
He spoke. We honored, we intoned
The memory of our heroic dead.
All that in passing. What force, I ask,
Bound every man to him alone?

His words came like a rapier's thrust.
And, pressing home a point, he struck
Out hard, his thumb hooked in his vest;
His foot swung slowly up and down.
His words could have been about crude oil,
And yet his arching frame was winged
With essential truth, his homely talk
Tearing at the husks of falsehoods
And man's obtuse illusion. His burr,
His words, which all men heard too well,
Were traced in the blood of great events.
He was their voice, their proclamation.
If he appealed to proven facts,
He knew that when he rinsed their mouths
With the logic of his simple words,
These became the pith of history.
Not wheedling, courting, but at ease
Before her face; always prepared
To question, study, and to goad,
He was her trusted confidant.
In envy only of the ages,
And jealous of their jealousy
Alone, he ruled the tides of thought,
And through that mastery—the State.
　1923

ABOVE THE BARRIERS

Poems of Various Years

The Drowsy Garden

The drowsy garden scatters beetles
Bronze as the ashes from a pan.
Level with me and with my candle
Hang flowering universes. Then,

As into some unheard-of faith
I pass the threshold of that night,
Where grizzled with decay, the poplar
Screens away the edge of moonlight,

Where lies the pond—an open secret,
Where billows of the apple sigh,
Where as a house on piles the garden
Holds up the mansion of the sky.

1914

Winter Skies

In a week, the starry river's one
Hard sheet of ice in dim blue light.
The skaters, tumbling, sprawl; the fields
Clink glasses with the sounding night.

Go easy, easy, eas-i-er, skaters,
Who cut your daring figures, and try
With grinding skates to grave at each turning
A constellation in a Norway sky.

The air and night seem chained with steel
Together. Beware, O skaters! You know
The night spreads far a copra's orbit
Around the earth, like a bone domino.

With howling of a dog frost-bitten,
The moon will freeze on iron heels,
And stuffed like liars' jaws with lava
Of breathless ice, each mouth congeals.

The Soul

As I now recall it, a jailbird set free;
And lest I forget it, a captive of time.
A spirit, a pilgrim, as many believe;
But for me, a shade from a homelier clime.

I may try to bury you under a stone
Of verses, in dust! But prisoned, you dwell
Sublime in your struggle, a true Tarakánova
When the river in springtime flooded her cell.

O Prisoner, pleading for pardon in gloom
And charging the times and guards at the bar!
While vanishing years fall away like leaves
By the garden hedge of our calendar.

The Urals for the First Time

In darkness, no midwife to help, pressing
Its hands against gloom, the Ural fastness
Half-dead with agony was screaming
In blindest pain at the birth of morning.

Tall ranges, loosed by chance, and the bronze
Of massive shadows came rumbling down.
A panting locomotive; the spectral fir trees
Swerved, stumbling, hurled by piercing shrieks.

An opiate, the smoky dawn. No doubt:
Plied by a huge flame-breathing dragon
To factories and mountain summits—
Like travelers duped by a practiced thief.

The flames of sunrise. From poppy-red skies
Like hunters on skis, they licked the foothills,
They suddenly lighted the firs with crowns,
And roused them to enter their kingdom again.

In glory arrayed, the shaggy dynasts
Of firs stood rank by rank, and trod
The orange velvet of carpeted snows
And tinseled cloth and damask.

Пронесшейся грозою полон воздух.
Всё ожило, всё дышит, как в раю.
Всем роспуском кистей лиловогроздых
Сирень вбирает свежести струю.

Всё живо переменою погоды.
Дождь заливает кровель жолоба,
Но всё светлее неба переходы,
И высь за чёрной тучей голуба.

Рука художника ещё всесильней
Со всех вещей смывает грязь и пыль.
Преображённой из его красильни
Выходит жизнь, действительность и быль.

Воспоминание о полувеке
Пронесшейся грозой уходит вспять.
Столетье вышло из его опеки.
Пора дорогу будущему дать.

Не потрясеньем и переворотом
Для новой жизни очищают путь,
А откровеньями, грозой и щедротами
Души воспламенённой чьей-нибудь.

Весна 1958,
Переделкино.

Б. Пастернак

Boris Pasternak sent the manuscript of his poem
The Passing Storm to Eugene Kayden in appreciation of Kayden's
translations of Pushkin, Lermontov, and Pasternak himself.
Mr. Kayden's translation appears as the last poem in this volume.

Spring Days

How many small buds like candle-butts
Fast glued to the boughs around!
Warm April days. The park has the savor
Of puberty, blaring with sound.

The forest is roped, in a noose of shrill
Small throats, as a lassoed buffalo,
And groans in the nets like a steely wrestler
In an organ throbbing with slow

Sonatas.—Oh, poetry, be like a sponge
With a suction pad that cleaves,
Drinks in, on a wet green bench in the garden
Alone with gummy young leaves.

Swell splendid with ruffles, lawns, clouds,
With trilling valleys converse.
At night I will squeeze your substance out
On thirsty white paper in verse.

Three Movements

1

When you probe each day for trifles,
Detail by detail, to the lees,
Then the sultry chatter of squirrels
Rings shrill in the resinous trees.

And languid, waxing in strength,
The pine trees drowse in a row,
While the forest boughs are peeling,
And their freckled sweat drips slow.

2

The garden's sick with miles of torpor.
The palsied hollows in their rages
Are fiercer far than hurricanes,
Than savage raids the tempest wages.

The storm draws near. The shriveled mouths
Of gardens taste dry nettles, fear,
Corruption, thatch. The cattle's bellow
Mounts in pillars of burning air.

3

Now the driven clouds in tatters
Grow on bushes in the groves.
Damp nettles fill the garden's mouth—
Smell of rain and treasure-troves.

No more wailing in the copses;
Now the air is clear on high.
Like a wading bird the blue
Walks barefoot across the sky.

And the oak and willow glisten,
And the bush is blossoming!
Like your moist and parted lips,
Like your tracks beside the spring.

Improvisation

I fed out of my hand a flock of keys
To clapping of wings and shrill cries in flight.
Sleeves up, arms out, on tiptoe I rose;
At my elbow I felt the nudging of night.

And the dark. And a pond, and the wash of waves.
And screeching black beaks in their savage attack,
All quick for the kill not to hunger and die,
While birds of the species I-love-you fall back.

And a pond. And the dark. The pulsating flare
From pipkins of pitch in the gloom of midnight.
The boat's keel nibbled by lapping of waves.
And birds at my elbow in their wrath and fight.

Night gurgled, washed in the gullets of weirs.
And it seemed if the young were unfed, by rote,
The hen-birds would kill—before the roulades
Would die in the shrilling, the crooked throat.

To a Friend

Come, don't I know that, stumbling in the dark,
Our night will never change to light again?
Is not the good of millions dear to me
Above the few, their petty good and gain?

And don't I make the Five-Year Plan my plan
And goal—sink with its fall, thrive with its rise?
Then why disown my private feelings, deny
Our great inertia, our doubts and fears despise?

In vain in our days of the Supreme Soviet
Where powers exercise their rightful choice,
They reserve the poet's chair in assembly halls:
He comes with wrath and passion in his voice.

To Anna Akhmátova

It seems I'm choosing the essential words
That I can liken to your pristine power.
And if I err, it's all the same to me,
For I shall cling to all my errors still.

I hear the constant patter on wet roofs,
The smothered eclogue of the wooden pavements.
A certain city comes clear in every line,
And springs to life in every syllable.

The roads are blocked, despite the tide of spring
All round. Your clients are a stingy, cruel lot.
Your eyes are moist from sewing by the lamp,
Where sunrise finds you bent above your work.

You long for the boundless space of Ládoga,
And hasten, weary, to the lake for change
And rest. It's little in the end you gain.
The canals smell rank like musty closet-chests.

And like an empty nut the hot wind frets
Across their waves, across the blinking eyelids
Of stars and branches, posts and lamps, and one
Lone seamstress gazing far above the bridge.

I know that eyes and objects vary greatly
In singleness and sharpness, yet the essence
Of greatest strength, dissolving fear, is the sky
At night beneath the gaze of polar light.

That's how I call to mind your face and glance.
No, not the image of that pillar of salt
Exalts me now, in which five years ago
You set in rhymes our fear of looking back.

But as it springs in all your early work,
Where crumbs of unremitting prose grew strong,
In all affairs, like wires conducting sparks,
Your work throbs high with our remembered past.
   1928

To M. T.

You're right to turn your pockets out
And say: "Well, rummage, feel, and search."
All's one to me why mists are damp.
Any fact would do—a day in March.

The trees in their soft overcoats
Stand planted in gamboge, secure,
Although the branches find for certain
The burden's painful to endure.

The branches shiver with the dews
Rippling like fleece upon merinos;
The dews run shuddering like hedgehogs
Bearing dry haycocks on their noses.

All's one to me whose talk and chatter
The winds from nowhere, blowing, bring,
What rumors muffled now in mists
I hear in every backyard spring.

All's one to me what kind of suits
The fashion holds to be in style.
The hearsays boxing in the poet
Like dreams will vanish in a while.

While rolling on through many channels,
By every fateful turn and bend
He'll drift like smoke from pit to pit
To another threatening dead end.

In sheets of steam he will rise through clefts
On top, though flattened in the heat,
And in the future men will say:
"His age was burning up like peat."
1928

Balzac

Paris exults in riches, business;
There rains, like vengeance, lull the air.
The pollen flies through sallow streets,
And wrathful bloom the chestnut trees.

The heat as with a glaze incrusts
The horses and the cracking whips;
Like peas piled in a sieve, the heat
Quivers in windows deep embrasured.

Tilburies rush in headlong flight.
Sufficient unto the day the hates:
Why fret about tomorrow's sunrise?
There wrathful bloom the nightmare trees.

But he, their debtor and their hostage,
Where is he hiding?—That alchemist!
As over books, his bulking figure
Curves over dusky alley slums.

He stretches like a poplar, puzzled,
As though to scan the ten commandments;
He spins for Paris, like a spider,
A rich commemorative mass.

He stares below, in agitation,
Spindle-shaped his wakeful eyes.
He spins like hempen fiber threads
The stories of Parisian haunts.

Should he negotiate his ransom
From the yoke of dreaded creditors,
Then he would fade to nothingness,
Watching thread on thread unwind.

What made him truly take on credit
Parisian crowds, the Stock Exchange,
The fields, the village unconstraint
At feasts among the willow trees?

He dreams of freedom like a valet,
A clerk who calculates his pension—
This man of massive mind, this man
Whose hands hang heavy as a mason's.

When will he wipe his sweat away,
Renounce the rot of coffee-houses,
And, fending off all care and thought,
Follow Saint Matthew chapter six?

1927

Sailing Away

We hear the lisping salt-sea drip.
Still mute and low the throbbing wheel.
Gently we take the harbor's shoulders
Past warehouses and twilight hill.

Wash-wash, wash-wash, the tideless waters.
The birch bark's sailing onward. Higher
The rollers, moaning, rush behind us,
Foaming pale-rose, on fire.

The crunch and crack of crayfish shells;
The birchen hiss in sunset glow.
The great sea mounts; bending, it shudders
With swelling tides below.

The shores recede in scrubby pines
And wretched groves to right and left.
In gloomy sluggishness sea waves,
Indifferent, regard our craft.

A billowing long roller strikes
The starboard dumb, and passes on—
To glide along the wooded beaches
To gather cloudberries in the sun.

About us still the shore line swims
To mark our voyage, and never strange
The shores we know. But not for long.
Our course grows menacing with change.

We take a dread half circle to
New tides and far-off boundaries:
The masts ride out between the gates
Of surging, racing open seas.

At last, the sea! And like an omen
Of storms and changes, suddenly
Above the grievous chasms, a gull
Drops like a stone, and scoops the sea.

The Gulf of Finland
1922

O Great Marksman

O great marksman, O vigilant hunter,
Phantom with a gun on the spirit's flood!
Spare me—one in a hundred—spare from
Crushing my life in your lust for blood.

Let me surmount a shameful death.
Hide me in willow and ice at night.
Start me at dawn from a lakeside brake.
Kill on the wing! But kill outright!

My thanks to you, O peoples disdained,
At our parting in my splendid flight!
I embrace in shyness friend and neighbor,
My country and kin in the hour of night.
   1923

Cocks

All night the water labored without a stop.
Till dawn the rain has burned its linseed oil.
In waves of lilac steam, the earth smokes like
A pot of cabbage soup that's near the boil.

But when the grasses, trembling, leap up again,
Who will my terror to the dew attest
As the first cock begins to crow, and then
Another, a third, and after him the rest?

And when the cocks from out the darkness call
Each in his turn, and probe each year by name,
Their crowing augurs clear the change to come—
To rain, to earth, to love, to each and all.

1923

Lilies of the Valley

Since dawn the day's grown hot. You part
The bushes, and the heavy noon
Will crack its leaden weight behind you,
And splinter from the diamond strokes.

It topples, edge-long, glittering,
In the retreat of trembling rabbits,
Like a heavy box of glass let fall
From sweaty shoulders to the ground.

White bodies canopied at night
Beneath these eaves appear coal black.
But spring's a fairyland of new
Incomparable loveliness.

The savage carnage of the heat
Stops at the edges of the grove.
You gaze at every birch you meet,
And they gaze back attentively.

But you have been forestalled. Someone
Is watching shyly near the ground:
A ravine lies studded by a shower
Of dew-wet lilies of the valley.

It lies, apart, with its suspended
Clusters of bells—a finger wide,
Or wide as two above the leaves,
One and a half above the roots.

The lilies ripple soundlessly,
Like kidskin, tender as brocade;
The shadows of the twilight grove
Receive them as their evening gloves.

1927

Lyubka

The rain came lately through this forest clearing
Like a surveyor's party. With tinsel threads
It weights the lily of the valley's leaves,
And water's in the mullein's furry ears.

These nurselings of the frosty firs pull down
Their ear lobes with the early evening dews;
They shun the day, prefer to grow apart,
And even waft their fragrance one by one.

And when at evening tea, in summer homes,
The mosquito's sails fill out with mist, and night,
Plucking the strings of a guitar by chance,
In milky darkness stands among the pansies,

The world grows sweet with evening violets:
The years and faces come to mind. And thoughts.
Each thing that may be rescued from the past,
And in the future granted us by Fate.

1927

SECOND BIRTH

Poems of 1932

Waves

All things will have their fullness here:
The past endured, the truth we now
Live by, our values, aspirations,
The truths of being I avow.

I greet the sea. The infinite.
The boundless sea in light, in gloom.
The mournful cadence. The surges bake
New waves like waffles of the foam.

They rove like sheep along the shore
In endless droves, forced by the still
Deep sky, that drove them out to pasture
And stretched itself along the hill.

In droves, rolled as in curving tubes,
My truths and subjects run to me
Along the runways of my anguish,
The crests of my grief and agony.

The waves run boundless, endless, charged
With change sublime, their destiny
In time unknown, but in their song
I hear the far-resounding sea.

I Would Go Home Again

I would go home again—to rooms
With sadness large at eventide,
Go in, take off my overcoat,
And in the light of streets outside

Take cheer. I'll pass the thin partitions
Right through; yes, like a beam I'll pass,
As image blends into an image,
As one mass splits another mass.

Let all abiding mooted problems
Deep rooted in our fortunes seem
To some a sedentary habit;
But still at home I brood and dream.

Again the trees and houses breathe
Their old refrain and fragrant air.
Again to right and left old winter
Sets up her household everywhere.

Again by dinner time the dark
Comes suddenly—to blind, to scare,
To teach the narrow lanes and alleys
She'll fool them if they don't take care.

Again the skies seize unawares
The earth; again the whirlwinds blow
And wrap the last few dozen aspens
Deep in a cloak of drifting snow.

Again, though weak my heart, O Moscow,
I listen, and in words compose
The way you smoke, the way you rise,
The way your great construction goes.

And so I take you as my harness
For the sake of raging days to be,
That you may know our past by heart
And like a poem remember me.

We Came to Georgia

We came to Georgia. You'll know this land
If hell you multiply by paradise,
Real want by tenderness, and if a hothouse
Might be a base supporting peaks of ice.

And then you'll understand what subtle doses
We ask of duty, work, success—and air,
United properly with earth and sky,
For man to be the way we find him here;

That he may rule himself in bondage, and
In famine, and in defeat, without a fault,
And thus become a model in the ages—
A man in sturdiness as plain as salt.

The Caucasus

The Caucasus lay vast in light.
It seemed a rumpled bed, the glow
Of azure ice more fathomless
Than chasms of stagnant heat below.

In mists and out of sorts, it reared
The hatreds of its icy crests
In steady automatic action,
Like salvos from machine-gun nests.

And gazing at this beauty, seeing
Brigades of labor in a race
To win new triumphs, how I envied
The obstacles they had to face.

Oh, if we had their sort of luck!
If, out of time, this age of ours,
This plan, might scrutinize our labor,
As this gigantic mountain lowers!

Then day and night before my vision
Our plan would march, its heel upon
The substance of my prophecies,
Shaping my life and my renown.

No time for angry altercation,
No time another hour to give
To writing verses, but, in secret,
My poems then I would really live!

Socialism

Here—now—our age of socialism!
Here in the thick of life below.
Today in the name of things to be
Into the future forth we go.

Like Gruzia shining in her beauty,
Like a land of light by open seas,
It beckons—veiled within a mist
Of wild surmise and theories.

There mothers of Putivl no more
Lament like cuckoos their dismay;
There joy no longer looks askance
In fear, but walks abroad by day.

There life and happiness converse
Together, free from hate and strife,
All joined to give their saving strength
And stay to every child and wife.

There men no longer by exchange
Compute the things they have or owe,
But gladly spend themselves in giving—
The all they have, the all they know.

Then let my message overtake
This wondrous age in history:
O may my children in their gladness
Out of the future answer me!

Don't Worry About Me

Don't worry about me, don't weep,
Do not torture your withering heart.
You live in my spirit, within me,
As my solace, my friend. Each part

Of my faith in the future is real,
Plain-spoken and free. Let us act,
Not saving our pride and illusions,
But honoring life in fact.

Away with your typhoid mattress!
Be a friend to the sun! Acclaim
As a brother the air, all your own
As a letter addressed in your name.

Burst on the world like a letter;
Correspond with horizons of air
In the language of Alpine spaces,
And conquer your pain and despair.

In your feast of skies and of lakes,
Of the marrow of mountain peaks,
You will learn I'm not a scribbler
Of words in the manner of freaks.

Good luck to you, dear! In your world,
Like a shoot growing straighter each day
In the sun—not under my roof—
You will judge in a different way.

Dear Love's a Heavy Cross

Dear love's a heavy cross at times,
But you are lovely, plain and free;
As true as any key to life,
The secret of your grace to me.

Spring comes with rustling in the night,
With living truth and tidings fair.
From such a fountain-head your race;
Your mind's impartial as the air.

To wake at ease, to find new sight,
Shake off the scum of idle chatter,
And live unspotted in the world—
No need for craft in such a matter.

Chin up, and Grin!

And still it snows! Chin up, and grin!
No matter, storm or rain in floods,
I'll make my darling's modest table
Rich with bitter poplar buds.

Let darkness drip its liquor now,
The soup, with cut up fennel sour,
The glasses dizzy with our clatter
And babble of the sweeping shower.

We should have punched the crazy snow,
And, deafened by our noise and play,
Unstopped the mouldy window frames
Like bottled wine, and hailed the day.

Bring in the noisy street! And damn
The weather! Take your ease from toil
And trouble now! Let sunlight flood
The salad dish with asphalt oil.

Then, behind Ilya's bumping chariot
Light-rumbling in the sky, I guess
My calflike ecstasies will gallop
Beside your calflike tenderness.

Darkness of Death

The darkness of death.
By the side of curbings
In ditches—the bodies
Of sunken roofs.

Sashes of cabins,
And the ochre of rooms
In a morgue of pools
As wide as streams.

There cabbies lie
And their painted carts,
And the fiery horses
Of faraway skies.

And raindrops on bushes
And a street in clouds,
The chirrup of birds
And buds on branches.

They come together,
Together with me,
Down desolate highways
To the Yamsky field.

Where lampposts drowse,
Where the azure's alien,
The bullfinches deafen
The air at dawn.

Once more the land
In meekness, in silence,
In her mighty labor
Offers her gifts.

Gay Shawls and Shoes

Gay shawls and shoes, the burning gaze
Of snowdrops round—they stir my blood!
Not flat with the water level runs
The rusty chocolate of mud.

The slush in sunlight kneads our spring
And the drowsy noise of stones, while sands
And streams will knead the call of birds
As cooks shape dumplings in deft hands.

Gay shawls and flounces—all in plenty!
The thawing earth's black liquorice.
I'll gain a hundredfold if I sigh,
And as a stream break free of ice.

And when I'm high above the level,
I'll thank you till I'm hoarse, yet deign
To sink your own true world, as in
A mirror, into my thanks again.

Put an end to curbs, an end to gutters
In spit and froth, an end to crowds,
To the crescent azure of the skies,
To empty shadows of the clouds,

To the gelatine of blind noon hours,
To yellow glass of pools, to lines
Of slender mica of the icefields,
And to hillocks girt by dusky vines.

The Fumes of Vain Renown

O Love, the fumes of vain renown
Are to me as pits of reeking flame.
But you are like a dictionary,
My source of secret, hidden fame.

But oh for stronger growth, deep down
Among the roots! . . . All talk apart,
In kinship true, I have my fame
And partnership in home-bred art.

Contemporaries not of poets,
The byways, lanes, and hedges rhyme
Our Pushkin now with snows and geese,
And Lermontov with summer time.

I wish the more that after death
When from this life we draw apart,
They may rhyme together you and me
Closer than auricle and heart.

May our tale of love that alters not
Proclaim our names, and never pass—
How as one we sucked the sap of life,
And will suck in aftertime the grass.

There Is No One in That House

There is no one in that house,
Only twilight. Only one:
Winter's in the drafty rooms
Where the curtains are undrawn.

Only grey cold damp is sweeping
In the emptiness below.
Only roofs, the snow; nothing
Besides the roofs and snow.

And the hoarfrost in the night
Comes with storms of winter near.
Conflicts of the long ago,
And the sadness of last year,

Sting my contrite heart with wrongs
And with unforgiven blame. . . .
Still my want of wood for burning
Will not spare the window frame.

Then the curtained door will shudder
Sudden with impending doom.
You will enter like the future,
Pace the silence of the room.

You will come inside my doorway,
Dear in something white, and plain;
Truly like a flake of snow,
Come in something white again.

You're Here at Last

You're here at last, a presence near
To me, to breathe the selfsame air
Again; near as our Kiev outside
The window, wrapped in sultry light;

As Kiev, restless in its sleep,
Striving, unconquered, by its will
To make the sweaty silken collar
Fall brick by brick from off its neck;

As Kiev, sweating in its leaves,
And free at last, with poplar trees
Along victorious avenues
Foregathered, weary, in a crowd.

Your mind and mien are like our Dnieper
Green-belted by its trails and groves;
You are my book of deep-down roots
And faithful entries day by day.

Today your presence is my call
At once to sit down by your side,
And, reading slowly from A to Z,
To write your presence in my book.

Vision of Tiflis

Twilight. The mettlesome hazels
In profusion spread. We beheld
In wonder a magic vista
And paused to gaze at the scene.

On precipitous falls, as ever,
Young woods were wantonly climbing
In sport uphill to the summit,
Trampling the rotting stumps.

The telegraph limped, crippled
As ever in its porcelain nests;
Air drifted, scrambling and panting
And tossing its wych-elms' braids.

Under shattered shadows of hazel
There, as ever, in looping array
The reddening highway wheeled onward
And twisted in evening dusk.

Every rise and fall warned of danger;
Every boulder, a lurking thief.
The buffalo, straining full tilt,
Sailed past like a naked devil.

In the sky, like serpents on eggs,
Clouds coiled in rings, more dread
Than the ranges of dragon shadows,
Than the forage of ancient Tartars.

The ranges were gravestones risen
On a background of snow-bound trails
Beyond the ethereal regions
Where Prometheus languished in death.

Like souls of the dead arisen
The glaciers in ranks appeared,
And the sun in India ink
Recorded the ghosts in its book.

Then we four on the hanging steep
Turned as one to gaze in the depths;
Like black spots on a hilt, below
Tiflis gleamed dark in a chasm.

It flouted the upper realms,
It mocked all creation, seeming
Like a tapered chimera below,
A city of a world unknown;

As though, surviving by tribute,
Its soul turned cold through the ages
When Tamerlane over the mountains
Led his hosts to battle of old;

As if evening laid bare on a plain
Its fortunes under Persian fire;
The roofs gleamed raspberry red,
And it swarmed as an ancient host.

Oh, Had I Known It Once for All

Oh, had I known it once for all
Before my career began, how chill
With death the lines of passion, how
They grip you at the throat and kill,

I would have pointedly refused
To mask by craft my secret aim.
We hesitate in doubt at first,
And dread the lure of sullen fame.

But age, like pagan Rome, instead
Of jests and twaddle and the lie
Mouthed in stagey lines, demands
The actor must in earnest die.

When passion is the play, it brings
To walk the stage a man unfree;
And then the lines are not of art,
But earth and life and destiny.

Hurry, My Verses, Hurry!

Hurry, my verses, hurry! Never
Have I so needed you before.
For there's a house where days are torn
Asunder in the heart's deep core,
Where work is ended, where they wait
And weep in helplessness their fate.

A bitter bromide there they drink
Like water, sleepless, and they sink.
You know—the house of bitter fare!
You know—be quick, and hurry there!

Let storms of winter whoop and stun,
Only hurry like a rainbow; run
Like a dream, a bit of cheerful news;
Because I love her—don't refuse!

Our women bear great miseries,
Saddled by ancient fetishes!
I know the crushing living pain
Of evil galling them to death!
Yet all my life I've choked my wrath
Against their meekness and their chains.
I say they are fooled by common lying
And tales of nature slow in dying,
That Bluebeard's real and stronger far
Than all my printed verses are.

And yet, unreal as Gogol's *Viy,*
It's still our frightful heritage,
A bogey, an offensive jest,
Enduring in our fantasy
As woman's fate from age to age,
Believed in fact among the best.

How brave she was, my love how fair!
And though beneath her mother's wing,
She gave her trust and childish glee,
Her days of peace unfearingly,
And, yes, her love! How fancy-free
She gave in play, unreasoning,
Her little world of trust and care!

When I Grow Weary

When I grow weary of their empty chatter
And turncoat flattery, my longing cries
For memories, my sunlight dreams—my life,
That I might gaze into its face again.

In ways unknown, and by its will alone,
I had the sense of exalted enterprise:
Not by my own desire or special gift
Or choice, but by my faith and ecstasy.

Then came the time of our constructive plans;
Winter again, the fourth year in its turn.
Two women, seared, in light of table lamps,
Like ghost-fires with their burdens gleam and burn.

We live in days to come, I tell them firmly,
And share one lot in common now. If crippled,
No matter! Stay. We are in fact run over
By the New Man in the wagon of his Plan.

And if from death no medicine will save us,
Then time, uncurbed, will rush more free into
The far unknown where the second Five-Year Plan
May long defer the thesis of man's soul

O do not mourn in vain! O do not grieve!
Despite my helplessness, I swear I'll stay
With you that day. The strong in hope endure
The plagues and suffering that bring them low.

ON EARLY TRAINS

The Poet

He appears. Long ages. Cloisters.
Somewhere torches are ablaze.
Who led hosts of warring peoples
Forth to greatness? . . . Far, in haze,

Centuries. New generations.
Later peoples in a stream.
He will whisper in their sluggish
Ears soft phrases of his dream.

"I am not a story-maker,
Nor with trifling warnings come.
Time will spare my style of writing
From your carping curry-comb.

"Are the gates of epochs closed,
Temples shuttered as before?
Yet my steed will reach your porches,
Reined in flight beside your door.

"I am not a ballad-babbler,
Not a strummer at your gate.
I will watch your ranks in battle
From a summit dark with fate.

"At a touch upon the bridle
Far my steed will bear me flying;
I will brave the desert spaces
Still in timeless darkness lying."

Like a thunderstorm enfolding
Death and passion, life and mission,
He will compass lands and spirits,
And deathless live in their tradition.

His advance, transforming nature,
Neath his hoofs of ringing steel
Will awaken barren places
And exalt such commonweal.

Cities, byways, huts and houses,
Every zone and market-place,
Every poplar, every doorway,
Soon will know him face to face.
1936

On Early Trains

This winter season of the year
I live near Moscow. Foul or fair
The day, in frost or snow, I go
By train to attend to my affairs.

I start at daybreak in good time
When there is not a speck of light,
And leave my creaking steps about
The quiet woodland trails of night.

Before me at the railway crossing
White willows on a barren rise;
The constellations flame on high
In gulfs of January skies.

Always ahead of me, on time,
The mail train and express arrive,
Or Number Forty overtakes me,
Before I catch Six Twenty-Five.

Sly wrinkles of dim light appear
Like feelers on a trembling stream
Of dark; the viaducts are stunned
By headlights in a sudden beam.

Inside the stuffy coach, seated
Among the plain and lowliest,
I fear I yield myself to feelings
I sucked in at my mother's breast.

But, brooding over past reverses
And years of our penury and war,
In silence I discern my people's
Incomparable traits once more.

And, worshipful, I humbly watch
Old peasant women, Muscovites,
Plain artisans, plain laborers,
Young students, and suburbanites.

I see no traces of subjection
Born of unhappiness, dismay,
Or want. They bear their daily trials
Like masters who have come to stay.

Disposed in every sort of posture,
In little knots, in quiet nooks,
The children and the young sit still,
Engrossed, like experts, reading books.

Then Moscow greets us in a mist
Of darkness turning silver-grey
When, leaving the underground station,
We come into the light of day.

And crowding to the exits, going
Their way, our youth and future spread
The freshness of wildcherry soap
And the smell of honeyed gingerbread.

1941

Summer Day

In springtime we prepare small fires
For gardens in the making,
With prayers for a summer harvest
The pagan altars waking.

In steam the virgin furrows glisten,
Prepared since early morning;
The earth's red-hot from end to end
Like a kitchen oven burning.

I throw my shirt aside—to work
Wherever labor takes me;
The heat bears down upon my back
And like wet clay it bakes me.

I stand with sunrays in my eyes
Beneath the noontide blazing;
From head to foot I'm like a pot
The potter's hand is glazing.

When dusk comes, darkling, in my room,
Within my sleeping quarters,
It fills me brimful like a pitcher
With lilac and with water.

Night wipes away the coat of heat
From cooling walls in shade,
And brings me forth, an offering
For any country maid.

   1941

Thrushes

Far at a lonely rural station
Deep silence falls on noontime plains.
Close by the railway line, goldfinches
Sing drowsily in dreamful lanes.

There boundless, burning as desire,
The highway stretches far in space.
A lilac woodland near looks like
A forelock of the cloud's grey face.

Along the wooded road the trees
Wave to the plodding horse in play.
Among the rotting stumps, in hollows,
Lie violets, leaf mould, decay.

No doubt the thirsting thrushes come
To drink in hollows such as these
When loud they sing the daylong tidings
With ice and passion in their knees.

In shrilling warnings long or short,
With trilling passionate or cold,
Their brass-lined singing throats are glossy
With puddles of the leafy mould.

They have their knolls and sheltered nooks,
Sly games of peeping through the blinds,
Their whispered fussing round the corners,
Their chatter, and feuds about their finds.

Daylong throughout their airy quarters
Their secrets flash in public rhyme.
Dark copses quaver long their chorus,
And branches sing in quarter-time.

Such is the thrushes' dreamful haunt.
They live in nature's homely brake
And wood, untamed, as artists should,
And theirs the way I too would take.

1941

The Tragic Story

A change will come. The capital,
Rebuilt, will live again.
But be forever unforgiven
The children's fear and pain!

There's no forgiveness for that fear
In faces seared and old.
For all its crimes the enemy
Shall pay a hundredfold.

We will remember cannonades,
And to the end condemn
The doers of the evil deeds
Like Herod in Bethlehem.

A brighter age will dawn. Our days
Are brief in history.
The grief of children maimed in war
Lives in futurity.

1941

THE VAST OUTDOORS

Early Winter Days

The door came open and the kitchen
Was filled with waves of frosty cold,
And, as in childhood on such evenings,
The world quite suddenly grew old.

Dry days and stillness. In the street
About five steps away, grey Winter
Stands timid in uncertainty
As one who doesn't dare to enter.

It snows, and all is new again.
Like blind old men without a guide
Or staff, the willows seem to wander
Into November space outside.

The stream's now ice; the osier freezes.
Above the naked ice looms high
The darkened overarching mirror
Of the infinite and vaulted sky.

But under it a birch tree leans
Beside the road; in loneliness,
With bright stars fastened in her hair
She gazes in that looking glass.

She long surmises, as her secret,
He brings surprises on the sly
To cottage folk, as wonderful
As are his wonders in the sky.

   1941

The Conqueror

Remember the dryness in the mouth
When, faced by a show of evil power,
We heard their savage bellowing,
And suffered in our trying hour.

But greater far than armor, justice
Was our defense, our course for good,
The fate incarnate in Leningrad:
A wall before the world she stood.

Remember our great deliverance,
The break in the besiegers' base!
The world upon her ramparts gazed,
In wonder gazed upon her face.

She bore on land and in the skies
The wars to death, in agony.
How bright her legendary fame,
Her day of immortal destiny!

   1945

Spring 1944

I shall never see a sweeter spring!
The sparrows are livelier and gay.
I do not even try to know
Why I am calm and glad today.

I work with a serener mind.
I hear the voice of liberty
In mighty octaves ring in choirs
From all the war-torn lands set free.

This tide of spring across the plains
Wipes clean away all winter traces,
And washes off the lines of care
And suffering in Slavic faces.

The grasses, panting, wait to burst
In light, and though the crooked alleys
Of Prague are still as graves, they too
Will sing like all the fields and gullies.

The soul of Czech and Serbian lands
Will wake with springtime tenderness,
And burst with flowers in the snow
Through shrouds of winter lawlessness.

Our fairy tales, long veiled in mist,
Revive like legends famed in story,
Portrayed in golden boyar chambers
And in Saint Basil's church of glory.

Our seers and dreamers in the night
Behold in Moscow their hope of good:
She is their home, the fountainhead
Of the world's new age of brotherhood.
　1944

DOCTOR ZHIVAGO'S POETRY

Hamlet

The plaudits die. I come on stage
Again. Leaning against the doorpost,
I strain to see afar in time
The fate that waits our present age.

Through thousands of binoculars
The darkness stares oppressively
At me. If possible, O Abba,
Father, let this cup pass from me.

I love Thy large design, and I
Would gladly act this role of woe.
But there's another play on stage;
Then spare me now, and let me go.

The acts are well thought out, the end
Foredoomed. Behold, I stand alone.
The Pharisees exult. How hard
This life, and long my way of stone.

Winds

I have died. You live alone with woe.
Now stormwinds, keening and repining,
Rock house and pine trees to and fro—
Not tree by tree, but at one blow
All groves and forests intertwining
With the illimitable space;
Thus sailboats sheltered at their base
Are rocked by winds along a bay.
But not in senseless agitation
The stormwind rages; day by day
About your grief its lamentation,
Its lullaby of desolation.

March

The earth is steaming, drenched in sweat;
Ravines run dazed and turbulent.
Like a bustling milkmaid hard at work,
Spring labors long, is well content.

The scanty snows now sick and helpless
Lie prone, with branching bluish veins.
The tines of pitchforks glow with health,
Freed from their winter rust and stains.

O nights, O days and nights! Plop-plop
The drops from eaves and window-sills,
The thinning icicles on gables,
The chatter of unsleeping rills!

The pigeons peck at oats in snow
About the barns and stables flung
Wide open, and vaster than spring air,
The smell of life-begetting dung.

Summer in the City

They whisper in silence.
With impetuous air
She sweeps up from her neck
Her tumbling hair.

Like a helmeted woman,
She peers out between
The encircling strands
That fall from her comb.

The night is seared
With its heat and grime.
The loiterers scamper
To get home on time.

From afar the thunder
Comes suddenly near,
And the window curtains
Flap trembling with fear.

Deep silence. The air is
Still muggy with heat;
Then flashes of lightning,
And scurrying feet.

When morning flames out
In a blaze again,
When the sun dries clean
The puddles of rain,

The lindens awaken
To a freshness deep,
Awaken sweet-scented
And heavy with sleep.

Winter Night

The snow was falling soft and slow
From land to land.
A candle flamed upon a table;
A candle flamed.

As midges of the summer swarm
Against a candle flame,
Outside the snowflakes swarmed against
The windowpane.

The blizzard modeled on the glass
White stars and arrows.
A candle flamed upon a table;
A candle flamed.

And soft along the ceiling lingered
Two flaring shadows:
Cross-folded arms, cross-folded legs,
And destiny.

Two little shoes fell to the floor,
Fell with a thud.
And soft the candle shed wax tears
Upon a dress.

The world lay soundless in the snow
Within the frosty night.
A candle flamed upon a table;
A candle flamed.

A draft then shuddered in the flame.
The fever of temptation,
It raised the cross of angel wings
Upon a wall.

Day after day through February
The snow came down.
A candle flamed upon a table;
A candle flamed.

Intoxication

Neath a willow with ivy entangled
We take cover in blustery weather.
My arms are wreathed about you;
In my raincape we huddle together.

I was wrong: Not ivy, my dear,
But hops encircle this willow.
Well then, let's spread in its shelter
My cape for a rug and a pillow.

Holy Week

The dark of night lies everywhere.
So young the night around,
We see how vast with stars the sky,
Each star as radiant as day.
And if the earth could have its way,
It would sleep on—through Easter Day—
Lulled by the reading of the psalms.

The dark of night lies everywhere.
So young the night, the square seems like
Eternity from end to end
Where still a thousand years must wait
The dawn of day and light.

The earth is naked to the bone:
It hasn't got a thread to wear
For swinging church bells in the night
Or singing with the choir.

From Maundy Thursday right up to
The eve of Easter Day,
The waters gnaw at riverbanks
And spin the waves in pools.

The woods are also naked,
And hushed through Passiontide;
The trunks stand crowded in a throng
Like worshippers at prayer.

And in the city, gathered near
The square, the thronging trees
Stand mother-naked too, and peer
Through gratings at the church.

They gaze with awe, and their alarm
And fears are justified:
The gardens leave their boundaries,
Degrees and laws of life are rent—
For a god is given to the grave.

They see the light at the royal gate,
The black pall, the tapers glowing,
And faces wet with tears.
They see the long procession starting
With Cross and Shroud,
And how two birches at the gate
Step aside to let them pass.

They move around the cloister walls
In crowds from curb to curb,
And bring into the church the spring,
The voices of the spring,
The heady fumes of spring,
The springtime of the year and air
Pungent as a holy wafer.

March scatters handfuls of the snow
Like alms among the lame,
As though a man stood in the portals
Holding the Ark, and opened it,
And gave its all unto the poor.

They sing and pray until the sunrise.
And having wept their fill,
Their chanting of the Psalms and Gospels
Flows with an air serene
On wastelands and on lonely lamps.

At midnight every kind of flesh
And creature hears in quiet
The voice of spring, believing
That when better weather comes
Death itself shall be destroyed
By the power of the Resurrection.

August

As sworn to, free and bountiful,
The sun has spread wide its morning rays
Abroad, and traced a saffron streak
From window curtains to my couch.

It spattered with its sultry ochre
The village cottages, the grove
Near by, my bed, my wet pillow,
The bookshelf, and a bit of wall.

I then remembered why my pillow
Became so damp with dew at night.
I dreamed you came to see me off;
You trailed behind me in the woods

In groups, asunder, and in pairs;
That someone in the crowd recalled
It was the holy sixth of August,
The Lord's Transfiguration;

That on this day Mount Tabor shines
In clear pure light without a flame;
That, as an oriflamme in brightness,
Autumn entices every heart.

You came through the beggared scrub,
Through sparse and stunted alder trees,
Then reached the coppice and the church
Bright-flaring as a ginger bunny.

The sky was like a next-door neighbor,
Sedate above unruffled treetops,
And far and away the air sang long
Of roosters interchanging calls.

Death hovered like a state surveyor
Inside the cloistered graveyard, scanning
Reflectively my lifeless face—
How best to dig my grave to size.

Each one, in every sense and feeling,
Heard inwardly the selfsame voice,
My prophetic voice of days ago
Resounding still with incorruption:

"Farewell, O skies of Transfiguration,
O gold of the Second Coming! Incline
To ease my grief in this fateful hour
With a last, a womanly caress.

"Farewell, O days of dull despair!
O woman, challenging all wrongs
And degradation, now we part!
I was your cause, your battlefield.

"Farewell, O winged imagination,
And daring flights in life made free,
And worlds made manifest in words,
In thought, in miracles of art."

Parting

He stands and stares across the hall
And does not know his home.
Her sudden leaving was a flight,
With chaos left behind.

He does not try to master why
The havoc of the rooms,
Because his headache makes him faint,
And tears obscure his eyes.

A throbbing pain rings in his ears.
Is he awake or dreaming?
And why so constant in his mind
The vision of the sea?

When you no longer see the world
Behind hoar-frosted panes,
The hopelessness of sorrow's more
Than the loneliness of desert seas.

And yet he drew her close to him,
One dear in every feature,
As the shore is closer to the sea
With each inflowing tide.

As reeds sink downward in a storm
With seas in agitation,
The form and grace of her sank deep
Within his secret soul.

Through many years of trial, days
Of utmost wretchedness,
Borne up by a tide of destiny,
She reached to him for help.

Amidst the endless obstacles
And perils of the sea,
The waves had borne her on, but near,
And nearer to him still.

And now her sudden flight—perhaps
Not by her choice at all.
This parting may bring on new grief
And suffering unto death.

He looks around this room again.
In the hurry of her leaving,
She turned each old familiar thing
In every drawer upside down.

He paces up and down in darkness,
He stoops, keeps putting back
The scattered scraps of sewing
And patterns in their places.

And having pricked his finger on
A needle in the cloth,
He sees the whole of her in life
And weeps in silence, softly.

Tryst

The snow will bury roads
And houses to the roofs.
If I go to stretch my legs,
I'll see you from my door.

In a light fall coat, alone,
Without overshoes or hat,
You try to keep your calm,
Sucking your snow-wet lips.

The trees and fences draw
Far back into the gloom.
You watch the street alone
Within the falling snow.

Your scarf hangs wet with snow,
Your collar and your sleeves,
And stars of melted flakes
Gleam dewy in your hair.

By the light of flaxen braids
I see your face, your scarf,
Your shape alone in the cold,
In that thin overcoat.

Flakes gleam beneath your lashes,
And sorrow in your eyes.
You were created whole,
A seamless shape of love.

It seems as if your image
Drawn fine with pointed steel
Is now in silver lines
Cut deep upon my heart.

Forever there your mind,
Your true humility.
It does not really matter
If the world is hard as stone.

I feel I am your double,
Like you outside, in dark.
I cannot draw the line
Dividing you and me.

For who are we, and whence,
If their idle talk alone
Lives long in aftertime
When we no longer live?

Star of the Nativity

It was wintertime.
The wind blew hard from the plain.
And the infant was cold in the cave
On the slope of a hill.

He was warmed by the breath of an ox.
The cattle huddled
Within the cave.
A warm mist drifted over the manger.

On a cliff afar the shepherds, awake,
Shook off the wisps of straw
And hayseed of their beds,
And sleepily gazed in the vastness of night.

They beheld the fields in drifted snows,
Gravestones and fences,
The shafts of a cart,
And a sky of stars above the graveyard;

And near them, unseen until then,
Like a watchman's candle
One star alone and shy
That shone on the road to Bethlehem.

At times it looked like a hayrick aflame,
Apart from God and the sky;
Like a barn on fire,
Like a farmstead ablaze in the night.

It reared in the sky like a flaming stack
Of straw and hay,
In the midst of a Creation
Amazed by this new star in the world.

And the flame grew steadily wider,
Large as a portent.
Then three stargazers
Hastened to follow the marvellous light.

Behind them, their camels with gifts.
Their caparisoned asses, each one smaller
In size, came daintily down the hillside.

And all new matters that were to come after
Arose as a vision of wonder in space.
All thoughts of ages, all dreams, new worlds,
All the future of galleries and of museums,
All the games of fairies, works of inventors,
And the yule trees, and the dreams all children dream:
The tremulous glow of candles in rows,
The gold and silver of angels and globes
(A *wind blew, raging, long from the plain*),
And the splendor of tinsel and toys under trees.

A part of the pond lay hidden by alders;
A part could be seen afar from the cliff
Where rooks were nesting among the treetops.
The shepherds could see each ass and camel
Trudging its way by the water mill.
"Let us go and worship the miracle,"
They said, and belted their sheepskin coats.

Their bodies grew warm, walking through snows.
There were footprints that glinted like mica
Across bright fields, on the way to the inn.
But the dogs on seeing the tracks in starshine
Growled loud in anger as if at a flame.

The frosty night was like a fairy tale.
And phantoms from mountain ridges in snows
Invisibly came to walk in the crowd.
The dogs grew fearful of ghosts around
And huddled beside the shepherd lads.

Across these valleys and mountain roads,
Unbodied, unseen by mortal eyes,
A heavenly host appeared in the throng,
And each footprint gleamed as an angel's foot.

At dawn the cedars lifted their heads.
A multitude gathered around the cave.
"Who are ye?" said Mary. They spoke: "We come
As shepherds of flocks, as envoys of heaven;
In praise of the Child and thy glory we come."
"The cave is too crowded. Abide ye a while."

Before dawnlight, in gloom, in ashen dark,
The drivers and shepherds stamped in the cold.
The footmen quarreled with mounted men;
Beside the well and the water trough
The asses brayed and the camels bellowed.

The dawn! It swept the last of the stars
Like grains of dust from the vaulted sky.
Then Mary allowed the Magi alone
To enter the cleft of the mountainside.

He slept in His manger in radiant light,
As a moonbeam sleeps in a hollow tree.
The breath of the ox and the ass kept warm
His hands and feet in the cold of night.

The Magi remained in the twilight cave;
They whispered softly, groping for words.
Then someone in darkness touched the arm
Of one near the manger, to move him aside:
Behold, like a guest above the threshold,
The Star of the Nativity gazed on the Maid.

Dawn

You were my life, my destiny.
Then came the war and ruin, too,
And for a long, long time I had
No word, no scrap of home from you.

Now after many, many years
Your voice stirs memories of pain.
All night I read your testament,
And rouse myself to life again.

I long to be with people, crowds,
To share their morning animation,
Prepared to smash to smithereens
Their wrongs and fears, their desolation.

And so each morning I run down
The stairs, at breakneck speed below,
As though this were my first release
To long deserted streets in snow.

The lights come on in cozy rooms.
Men drink their tea, and hurry down
To trolley lines. Within an hour
You'd hardly recognize the town.

The blizzard weaves its nets of snow
Around the gates. In each family,
To get to work on time, the men
Gulp down their porridge and their tea.

My heart goes out to each and all,
To everyone who feels he's down;
I melt myself as melts the snow,
And as the morning frowns, I frown.

As wives, as children, or as trees,
These people are a part of me:
They rule my life, and by that sign
I know my sole true victory.

The Miracle

He walked to Jerusalem from Bethany
With forebodings and grief in His heart.

The thorny scrubwood lay scorched by the sun.
No smoke from a hut or hostelry near;
No breeze in the reeds. And the air was hot
By the moveless, glassy, quiet Dead Sea.

With a few small clouds in fellowship,
He wearily walked in the dust of day
With bitter pain by the bitter sea
To be again with His own disciples.

So deep in loneliness, brooding, He moved.
The desert smelled in sadness of wormwood.
The world lay still. He stood in the midst
Of the desert alone. The land lay prostrate
As though in a faint. The heat, the desert,
Dry springs, and lizards wearied His mind.

He beheld a fig tree rise in the way,
With branches and leaves, but He found no fruit.
And He said unto it: "Of what profit thou?
What joy can I have in thy fruitless life?

"I thirst and hunger, but thou art barren.
Thy greeting is worse than stumbling on stone.
How empty, how senseless thy life in my sight!
Stay barren forever to the end of time."

A shudder ran down the tree at that curse,
As a spark of lightning runs down a rod.
And the fig tree instantly withered to ash.

But if roots and trunk, if branches and leaves
Had had their freedom and choice at that hour,
Then nature's laws might have come to their aid.

But a miracle is a sign—an act of God.
In days of confusion, at a call unforeseen,
We stand, unprepared, before God our Lord.

Earth

Spring rushes like a roaring tide
Even in exclusive Moscow homes.
The moths come fluttering from closets
And settle into summer clothes.
The furs are packed away in trunks.

Along the wooden balconies
Bright flowerpots appear in rows
Showing off their gillyflowers.
Rooms have the free-and-easy look
Of spring, and attics smell of dust.

The alleys shout hail-fellow greetings
To every mole-eyed window frame.
White night and sunset by the river
Just cannot keep apart in passing.

And you can hear in every hallway
What's going on all day outside,
Or overhear gay April gossip
In secret with the dripping eaves.
He knows a thousand, thousand stories
About plain people and their sorrows.
Sunrise and evening red grow cold
Along the fence, while they still talk.

There is the selfsame eeriness
And heat in streets and living rooms;
Even the air feels not the same.
The selfsame lacy willow twigs,
The selfsame burgeoning white buds
At crossroads, under window sills,
In workshops, and in sunny streets.

Then why do the vistas weep in mists?
Why bitter the smell of soil and dung?
But that's just what my mission's for—
To keep the great outdoors from boredom,
And lands beyond the city bounds
From grieving in their loneliness.

That's why in early spring my friends
And I foregather in the night,
Why parting brings a sadness on,
Why friendly feasts are testaments—
That our tides of suffering might burn
Away the cold in the heart of man.

Evil Days

When He came to Jerusalem
In the week before the feast,
He was hailed by loud hosannas,
And with palms unto His glory.

But days grew frightful and savage;
Men's brows became knit with disdain,
Their spirits unmoved by compassion.
And then came the postscript, the end.

The heavens lay heavy as lead,
With heaviness crushing the houses.
The Pharisees came after proof,
And wheedled like sly old foxes.

He was thrown to the scum by forces
Of evil supporting the Temple.
With the selfsame zeal they had lauded
His name, they cursed Him at last.

The rabble from the neighborhood
Gathered to peer in the gateways;
They jostled forward and backwards
Expecting the worst for Him.

The alleys whispered their rumors,
And the squares their secret talk.
He remembered the flight to Egypt
And His childhood as if in a dream.

He remembered the silent desert,
The majestic mountain top
Where Satan had tempted Him
With the kingdoms of the world.

And the marriage feast at Cana,
And the guests who gazed in awe,
And the sea whereon He had walked
To the boat as along dry land.

And the poor who met in a hovel,
His descent to the cave with a light;
How, frightened, the candle fluttered
When Lazarus rose from the dead.

Mary Magdalene

I

As soon as night descends, my demon
Walks beside me. That is the price
I must pay for all my past, my old
Dark memories tearing me to pieces
When I, a slave to the whims of men,
Lived like a fiend, a wanton fool,
The street my shelter in this life.

I have but a few scant minutes left
Before the silence of the grave,
Before the end. But while there's time
I shatter at Thy feet my life
As a precious alabaster vessel.

Oh, what would my existence mean
To me, O Master, O my Saviour,
If eternal life were not the life
Awaiting me at my table at night,
Like a late new visitor allured
Into the net of my profession.

But do make plain to me the truths
Of sin and death, hell, brimstone fire,
If I have grace, if I have come
To be through faith a part of Thee,
Even as branch and tree, when now
My heart is infinite with grief.

When I embrace Thy feet, O Jesus,
When dear I hold them in my lap,
I feel I am learning to embrace
At death the wooden beam, Thy Cross,
And, fainting, in my grief prepare
Thy body for the burial.

Mary Magdalene

II

Our women clean the house before
The holy feast. Aloof from their work,
With myrrh and spikenard from a bowl,
I will anoint Thy most pure feet.

I'm looking, Jesus, everywhere to find
Thy sandals. I'm blinded by my tears.
My hair has fallen like a pall
In loosened coils before my eyes.

I have set Thy feet upon my lap
And washed them, Jesus, in my tears.
I have wound them with my own necklace,
I dried, I hid them in my hair.

I see the future clear, as though
The years stand still by Thy command,
And I can prophesy events
Like ancient sibyls in a trance.

The veil will tremble in the Temple,
Rent in twain. We will closely stand
And wait in fear. The earth will rock,
Perhaps out of pity just for me.

The watchmen will be changed again,
And soldiers will be riding forth.
Like waters springing in a storm
Thy Cross will strive to reach the sky.

I shall lie prostrate, faint before
The Crucifix, and bite my lips.

Thy arms, O Lord, upon the Cross
Embrace too many in the world.

For whom Thy life, Thy open arms,
For whom such agony, such power?
Are there so many souls to save,
So many hamlets, rivers, woods?

Three days of agony shall pass,
Three days in frightful emptiness,
But I shall in my faith behold
The day of Resurrection come.

Garden of Gethsemane

The turn along the road was shining bright
In the regardless glimmer of far-off stars.
The road circled around the Mount of Olives,
And lower, in the valley, the Kedron ran.

A narrow meadow steeply dipped halfway,
And at its end the Milky Way began.
The silvery grey olives, straining forth,
Appeared to stride upon the empty air.

Beyond the meadow was someone's garden plot.
He left His disciples by the stone wall, saying:
"My soul is very sorrowful, even to death;
Tarry ye here, and watch alone with me."

He had refused, at His free will, the power
To work miracles, to have dominion over life,
As though these powers were His as grants on loan.
And now He stood as mortal men, even as we.

The boundless space of night seemed as a span
Of non-existence and annihilation.
The universal sphere was like a soundless waste,
And only the garden spot was warm with life.

And, peering far into the black abyss
All void, without beginning or an end,
He prayed, the while His body sweated blood,
"My Father, let this cup pass from me."

He eased His deathly weariness with prayer.
He left the garden. He came to His disciples.
He found them in the wayside grass, asleep,
Their eyes grown heavy and their bodies weak.

He wakened them: "God hath chosen ye to live
While I am in the world, yet ye sprawl like dead.
Behold, the hour is at hand, and the Son of Man
Delivers Himself into the hands of sinners."

And while He spoke, lo, by surprise arose
A throng of slaves, a mob of vagrant men,
With swords and torches, and Judas at their head
With a betraying kiss upon his lips.

And Peter drew his sword and smote the ruffians;
He struck a servant down, cut off his ear.
But Jesus said: "Put up thy sword again.
The way of life is not the way of steel.

"And dost thou think my Father would not send
In my defense His hosts of winged legions?
That, never harming even an hair of mine,
My enemies would not flee before my face?

"Behold, the book of life is open at a page
Of greater price than the holies of the past.
The written words shall be fulfilled at last,
And the future come into the world. Amen.

"The passing of an age is like a parable,
And in the passing it will burst in flame.
In the name of its awful splendor I will,
In my voluntary passion, suffer death.

"I will suffer death and on the third day rise
Again. Like rafts descending on a river,
Like a caravan of sails, the centuries
Out of the night will come to my judgment seat."

IN THE INTERVAL

Fame

It's unbefitting to be famous
And say fame elevates our souls;
It's unbefitting to trouble over
Your notes and manuscripts and rolls.

The way of art is self-surrender,
Not born of praise or great success.
How shameful when your name's a byword;
Your labor—vain and meaningless!

Oh, live! Not as pretenders live—
In emptiness, with many fears,
But give your heart to vast horizons
And hear the call of future years.

Leave out the faceless present, leave
Whole chapters out! Deliberate
The matter nearest to creation—
The themes of freedom, life, and fate.

Then pass into your deep seclusion,
A man alone and unespied,
As vanishes in evening mist
And sudden dark the countryside.

Another, step by step, will follow
After, and enter your retreat,
But you yourself must not prefer
Your victories to your defeat.

You must never violate your purpose
One jot, one atom, to survive.
But be alive—this only matters,
Alive, to the end of ends alive!
    1956

Summer in the Country

A ghost is roaming through our cottage,
And flits across the attic floor.
A goblin roams about the rooms,
Along the ceiling, at the door.

He bobs up in his awkward manner
And gets in everybody's way;
He blows the napkins off the table;
He flutters in our shirts at play.

With muddy feet he rushes in
On gusts of wind along the hall;
He clasps the curtains like a dancer
And whirls them wildly up the wall.

But who's that batty, trifling ninny,
That ghost, that country egotist?
No, he's our lodger of the summer,
That freakish exhibitionist!

He makes our cottage his possession,
In fee, while he enjoys his rest,
July of country air and thunder—
July's our tenant, boarder, guest.

July that lugs about his person
The burr and dandelion fluff;
July that scampers through the windows
And chatters loudly in a huff!

That tomboy, good-for-nothing sloven
Who smells of fennel, lime, and rye,
Of dung and mulches, beets and grasses,
That meadow-scented month July!

1956

Autumn Days

The highway. Ditches. Woods.
We wander off in light
After mushrooms, and we mark
The mileposts left and right.

We leave the open highway.
We scatter, ranging through
The forest gloom; we ramble
Ankle-deep in dew.

Through thickets deep in dark
The spears of sunlight rush
On brown and yellow mushrooms
Under every bramblebush.

They hide among the stumps
Where birds alight to rest,
And when we lose ourselves,
The shadows guide our quest.

So brief these autumn days
And sunset solitudes,
The twilight has no chance
To linger in the woods.

Our bags and baskets burst
With gathered stock before
We leave for home: pine mushrooms
Make almost half our store.

Behind our backs the dark
Still forest walls arise,
And, beautiful in death,
The day flames bright and dies.
   1956

First Snow

The snowstorm whirls in swarming flakes
Shrouding one and all—
The paper stall and paper girl
Under a downy pall.

It seems, from long experience,
None will dare deny
The snow is born of secrecy
Only to mystify.

He tricks you out, sly reprobate,
He turns you fair and white,
And brings you from some frolic home
Far too late at night.

While roads are blinded by the storm
And dazed with hoar,
A shadow staggers near the house
Groping for the door.

It moves about unsteadily,
And for all I know
Someone has some misdeed to hide
Deep down in snow.

The snowstorm whirls; in fear each pane,
Each fence and stake.
The web is woven white and whole,
Difficult to break.

   1956

Hayricks

Dragonflies flit in blazing darts,
Bees wing unendingly, the blithe
Farm girls halloo atop the wagons,
And reapers stride beneath their scythes.

And while the sunny weather holds,
They rake the fodder turning brown;
They stack it deftly into ricks,
Like houses, till the sun goes down.

Each rick in evening dusk assumes
The likeness of a lodging hut,
Where night lies down to rest upon
A bunk of clover freshly cut.

At break of day the hayricks loom
Like lofts in ashen morning light,
Where the harvest moon has dug itself in
While stopping over for the night.

At early dawn cart after cart
Rolls creaking on in murky air
In twilight fields, and day crawls out
Of bed with hayseed in its hair.

Again the sky shines blue, again
Ricks rise as clouds in the noon hour.
Like vodka steeped with aniseed,
The earth lies sweet and vast in power.
1956

Hail All Things Glad

The lake is one enormous saucer.
The sky—a multitude of clouds
Like piles of mountain glaciers risen
Immovably in dazzling crowds.

In veering daytime light the woods
Seem new and changeful, not the same:
One moment deep in murky shadows,
On a sudden like a torch aflame.

When, after days of stormy weather,
Between the clouds looks out the vast
Blue sky, how festive in their triumph
The lowly grass and fields at last!

The winds lie still in calmer air;
The sun is kindred to the grass;
The leaves in light transparent glisten
Like figures etched in colored glass.

And in the windows of the church
True prophet, saint, and holy wife
In shining crowns, unsleeping, keep
Their vigil with eternal life.

I feel the universe is one
Cathedral infinite with calm,
And that I hear the mighty choirs
Ring out in one triumphant psalm.

O World, O Life, immortal Time!
I will now in secret adoration
Live, trembling, faithful in thy service
With tears of joy and exaltation.

1957

Autumn Woods

The autumn wood's grown hairy,
With calm and shadows deep;
No woodpecker, squirrel, owl,
Now wakes it from its sleep.

By autumn trails the sun
At twilight enters it,
Looks warily about
In fear of a snare or pit.

Here swamps and moss abound;
Here tangled alders glow.
Beyond the forest marshes
A cock begins to crow.

Again, again it crows,
Then stops for very long,
As though to ponder why
The morning needs its song.

But soon another cock
In some far village yard
Takes on the challenger
Like a sentryman on guard.

Cock after cock sings loud
With still increasing zest,
Their outcries pointing north
Or south, then east or west.

The trees lean out to see
How wide the fields, how new
And vast the world beyond,
How infinite the blue.

1957

In the Hospital

They crowded, blocking the sidewalk
As before a window display;
They watched the stretcher uplifted
And the ambulance speed on its way.

Past houses, markets, and loungers
At corners, it shrilled in the night;
It hurled in confusion, in courses
Of darkness, two arrows of light.

Militiamen, crossings, and faces
Bobbed up in the light of the car;
The first-aid attendant was swaying
With her kit and ammonia jar.

The gutters drearily pattered
With rain at the entrance; the age
And the case of the patient were scribbled
On line after line on a page.

He was left on a cot in the hall,
For the ward was full at that time.
The hall was drafty; the passage
Oppressive with iodine.

A window held bits of a garden,
And with it a part of the sky.
He studied the beds and the sick
And the bustling attendants nearby,

When, catching a nurse's attention,
He suddenly knew in his pain
That hall and enclosure would never
Return him to freedom again.

Thankful, he turned to the window
And faced a great wall outside
That reflected the lights of the city
In their changeful, smouldering tide.

The lights of the avenues glimmered
In the shuddering flames of the sky;
A branch of a maple in tatters
Was waving to bid him goodbye.

"O Lord!" he sighed in his sorrow,
"How perfect the works of Thy hand!
The beds and the walls, my passing
In death, the night in the land.

"I swallow a sedative capsule;
I weep in my desolate place.
O Father, my tears and my torments
Keep me from seeing Thy face!

"How sweet Thy light to my spirit,
At the end in my agony;
How sweet that my lot and being
Are Thy gift of life unto me.

"And, dying, I feel that Thy hands
Are ablaze, that I die in Thy grace,
That I rest, O Lord, in Thy keeping,
Like a priceless ring in a case."

1957

The Linden Alley

A manor of uncommon beauty,
An arching gateway, solitude.
Set in a dark cool park, it rules
Rich meadows, fields, a distant wood.

Here massive linden trees, their crowns
In secret councils met, as peers
Remember in the shadeful alley
Their past two hundred rooted years.

And underneath their vaulted branches,
Along symmetric passages
Lie lawns and plotted flowerbeds
Gay in their summer gala dress.

No sunny patterns on the sands
Beneath the ancient trees attend
The dim long tunnel of the alley,
The brightness shining at each end.

But, in the time of blossoming,
The fenced-in trees as in a tent
Of pillared shadows spread about
An overpowering magic scent.

Here visitors, in summer dress,
While strolling in this wonderland,
Enjoy the unfathomable sweetness
Which only bees can understand.

This gripping fragrance is the garden's
Great truth and essence if we look
For truth. The lawns and flowerbeds
Are like the covers of this book.

Like waxen candle-lights, the flowers
Transfiguring each linden tree,
Above the manor house flame bright
In leaping tongues of ecstasy.
　1957

Ploughing Time

So unfamiliar, new! And who
Can tell the fringe of skies revealed
From lands below? Like chessboard squares
Each furrowed and unbroken field.

The harrowed fields lie vast and trim
Spread level on the plains about
As though the valleys had been swept,
Or else the hillocks flattened out.

On these days, too, outside the furrows,
As one in mind, unitedly
The downy trees burst into leaf
And reach out skyward, tall and free.

No speck of dust on a single maple,
And nowhere are the hues as bright
And pure as those on silver birches,
Or on the fields in haze of light.

   1958

The Passing Storm

The air is heavy with the passing storm.
The earth lies calm and free and glad again.
Through all its pores the flowering lilac bush
Drinks deep the pure cool freshness of the plain.

The world's reborn, transfigured by the storm.
The gutters shed a flood of rain. Now fair
And vast the blue beyond the shrouded sky,
And bright the ranges of celestial air.

But more exalted far the poet of power,
Who washes clean away the dust and grime,
When by his art emerge transformed the harsh
Realities and truths of naked time.

For then our lifetime sorrows with the storm
Retreat. Free from the past of tutelage,
Our century proclaims the hour has come
To clear a passage for the future age.

No swift upheaval swelling of itself
Can make the way for our new age to be;
Our hope—the message of a spirit kindled
By truth revealed and magnanimity.
 1958

Notes and Comments

page 3. *About My Verses.* Daryál, the great gorge in the Caucasus through which the Terek River flows, is the scene of Lermontov's best poetry. Lermontov (1814–41) was one whom Pasternak has admired most from his early youth. From him he learned that poetry must be expressive, true to life experience, but also faithful to eternal values. In *My Sister Life* (1922) Pasternak found himself in his own truthful, unique forms of expression. Lermontov's Demon, although a symbol of defiance and rebellion, was not altogether a Byronic rebel, but had Russian birthmarks. His revolt was interfused with melancholy, awareness of the tragedy of existence, and yearnings for love and peace and perfection in the universal order. "What century have we outside" was not a query prompted too seriously in a spirit of complete indifference to social affairs. Pasternak soon realized that the poetic imagination cannot remain aloof and indifferent to the dimensions of time and historic life, that the poet cannot evade his own age by escape from dead time ("To M. T."), and that he cannot shut out or transcend history without a sense of betrayal and guilt ("There Is No One in That House").

page 13. *Definition of Poetry.* Pasternak does not speak dogmatically about poetry, but gives instead a series of separate images of poetry. One of the definitions (the cry of a world at birth) may seem like a willful translation of the original text which says "tears of the world on a shoulder" (*v lopátkakh*). However, in many regions of Russia common people speak of unshelled peas or beans in their pods as being *v lopátkakh*. Correctly interpreted, it means then that poetry is the expression of the birthpangs of the new in the world.

page 22. *Moochkap.* The name is that of a remote village at at a small railway station in Tambov Province of central Russia. The watchful, excited mind of the observer and the details of the physical environment are intertwined, so that the effects are both visual and emotional.

page 23. *Summer 1917.* Spiritual and physical details are

blended in this poem as in a landscape painting. The poet accepts the Revolution as an event inherent in nature and in the soul of the common people, and he states that all classes, including the land-owning gentry, were touched by the magic of new ideas of social harmony and dreams of brotherhood. In another poem, "So Be It," the Revolution is represented as coming like a rifle shot, like an eruption of nature, yet the poet is confident that the new day is a source of vitality and hope. His confidence in the new man, despite his vulgarity and insolence, is asserted in "January 1919," wherein the poet accepts the new with patience and humor and wisdom, in the belief that peace comes from men as it does from nature. In "Sailing Away" and in "We Are Few" the adventure into the unknown future, beyond established usage and institutions, finds an almost epic treatment.

page 36. *The Racing Stars.* The central subject of the poem is the composition of Pushkin's "The Prophet." The imagery is original and consistent. The poem is begun at night, within four walls of a room, and completed at dawn. But the setting is of world-wide, cosmic dimensions. The listening Sahara represents the growing consciousness of the poet; the smile of the wilderness, the joy of creative energy as the night wears away; the snoring Arkhangelsk, the poet's indifference to everything about him; dawn, the symbol of final achievement. These elements on both literal and symbolical levels are fused into one poetic act resembling the creative forces of nature itself. Pushkin's "The Prophet," a translation of which follows, has a large place in Russian literature and social thought.

> My soul athirst for holy grace,
> I wandered lone on desert ways,
> And lo, there rose before my face
> The angel of the Lord of Days.
> He touched my eyes with fingers light
> And soft as sleep at eventide;
> My eyes became with vision wide,
> Alarmed as eagles in the night.
> He laid his finger on my ears,

And I heard a tumult fill the sky,
The sweep of angel wings on high;
I heard the trembling of the spheres,
The sap within the vines and trees,
And reptiles moving under seas.
He leaned above my mouth awhile
And tore from me my tongue of lust
And all its vanity and guile,
And with his bloody hand he thrust
Between my lips unmurmuring
And cold the serpent's subtle sting.
And with his sword he clove my breast,
And plucked my heart of fear and care,
And in my bosom rived and bare
A coal of living flame he pressed.
I lay upon the waste as dead.
And God called unto me and said:
"Arise, O prophet! Hear and see!
Fulfill my will, go forth again!
In every land, by every sea,
Burn with my words the hearts of men!"

page 42. *Thus Life Begins.* Few poets have dared to express in a brief lyric, on a high level of symbolism, the fate of human beings from childhood to maturity under modern industrialism where the humble are beset by fears and anxieties, exploited by self-assertive careerists and adventurers. True, creative energies (poetry) set them on their way, but it often means a defiance of eternal values, while we give lip service to the Son of Man. Shelley, too, raised this issue in his unfinished *The Triumph of Life.* In his dream he watched the passage of great leaders and world conquerors—"hoary anarchs, demagogues, and sage"—and heard Rousseau say that "their power was given but to destroy."

page 45. *In the Wood.* Poets often set love against the dread of fleeting time. But Pasternak holds that the two categories of experience and time are not divided in the organic structure of life. In this poem, the two lovers, on a physical plane, are in a state of satiety bordering on sleep. They are insensible to time, yet time persists in fact. Therefore, the poet constructs time symbolically. While the lovers sleep dreamlessly, the forces of nature construct a clock of their own, within the ether. In this manner we have the total fusion of nature, the lovers and the infinite beyond in a single unity. The poem is both metaphysical and sensuous. Nature and poetry are thus welded together by subjecting nature to the discipline of poetry.

page 48. *I've Come from the Street.* The poem may be taken as an epitome of Pasternak's method and thought. He builds, like a musician, a counterpoint of different sensuous themes—visual, auditory, and emotional—such as poplar, house, air, a story begun by a star, and his own feelings about people. The central theme is that we live today in an ailing culture, in crumbling houses; that the story first begun by a star and once heard by man is now broken off; that we are in confusion, empty of mind and thought. These themes are not treated in absolute isolation, but they are joined together by a romantic note about the poplar tree that stands "amazed" at the sight of unnatural, alienated man.

page 55. *Bloody Sunday.* This event marked the start of the Revolution of 1905. The government made use of security police and secret agents, especially the priest Gapon, popular among workers as a missionary and an eloquent speaker. To discourage independent political activity, he secretly organized groups of workers with monarchist leanings. At his suggestion, the striking workers organized a mass procession to the Winter Palace to lay a petition for redress before the Tsar. The workers were crushed by Cossack and infantry units with sabres and gunfire, leaving more than 1,000 dead and over 2,000 wounded. That event opened the way to terroristic acts. The Tsar's uncle, Grand Duke Sergéi Aleksándrovich Romanov (mentioned in the poem), governor general of Moscow and patron of the secondary school attended by young Pasternak, was killed by a bomb thrown by the socialist revolutionary I. Kalyáev.

page 59. *Mutiny at Sea.* The Revolution of 1905 spread rapidly among the sailors of the Black Sea fleet. The revolt began on the battleship "Potémkin," where on June 27 the sailors were served stale food and wormy meat. The leaders were condemned to suffer severe discipline, but the crews liberated them, shot several officers, raised the red flag, and placed themselves under the command of sailor Afanási Matushénko. The red commander directed the battleship to Odessa, where workers were engaged in street fights with police and troops.

page 65. *A Testament.* Lieutenant Piótr Petróvich Schmidt (1867–1906) was the central figure at the sailors' uprising at Sebastopol in 1905. He was popular because of his democratic convictions and earnest dedication to liberal causes. The crews, including some infantry units, supported the workers at the naval base and in the city itself in the struggle with the military. On November 27 Lieutenant Schmidt went aboard the cruiser "Ochákov," intending to place himself at the head of the entire fleet, but only a few units raised the red flag; the shore batteries remained loyal and fired on the rebel ships. Together with three other sailors, Schmidt was condemned to death by a military tribunal and shot on March 19 on the island of Berezan. The personality of the officer and the sea mutiny of the fleet inspired several writers and poets.

page 66. *Sublime Malady.* Pasternak once said that the poet must not distrust the living voice of life and truth, that art is like a sponge applied to the pattern of the race, that it continues the image of the race. This poem is a concentrated dramatic sketch of the epic that was the Revolution of 1917. It particularly reveals the failure of the conservative, liberal, and intellectual elements in a time of crisis. Pasternak condemns his own class of liberal thinkers who had no feeling for the image the masses had of themselves. He proudly embraces the positive leadership of men who acted as master builders, who opened the windows upon the future. The poem ends with an evocation of Lenin as thinker and leader; he is referred to as *he* reverently—a man so great that he does not need a name.

page 79. *The Soul.* The description of the soul as a true

Tarakánova has reference to a historic personage, Princess Tarakánova, who challenged the legal right of Catherine the Great to the throne. She died a prisoner in a fortress when her cell was flooded by the rising waters of the Neva.

page 85. *To a Friend.* Pasternak sees the poet as a force in national deliberative assemblies, as the people's spokesman, as a challenger to whom art and the practical life are undivided. In poetry and prose, Pasternak asserts the right of spiritual man to be "the voice of truth" without false idealization. He likes to quote Shakespeare's line about "art made tongue-tied by authority" (Sonnet LXVI). The state, demanding man's complete allegiance, must be faced by the poet who has an understanding of the totality of human values and experience. In fact, the state is faced with the poet in every man, because every man possesses his own uniqueness as a personality.

page 86. *To Anna Akhmátova.* This name is the pseudonym of Anna Arkádyevna Gorénko (b. 1888). Her love lyrics, published in 1912–15, established her universal reputation. Together with the poet Nikolai Gumilev, she became the leader of the Acmeist school of poetry, a movement founded in opposition to symbolist vagueness and mysticism. With the publication of her *Anno Domini* (1922), she practically closed her literary career, except for her studies of Pushkin, selections from her poetry books published in 1940, and a few patriotic poems in 1950. In the literary purge of 1946 Akhmátova's work was condemned, labeled as decadent and harmful to Soviet youth. The reference to the "pillar of salt" (stanza 7) is to Akhmátova's poem, "Lot's Wife"—the woman who paid with her life for taking one glance back, in her great compassion for perishing humanity, upon the city which was her home.

page 88. *To M. T.* The poem refers to Marina Ivánovna Tsvetáyeva (1892–1941), a major poet of the 'twenties. Her style was extraordinary, dynamic, staccato in its rhythms. An opponent of Bolshevism, she emigrated in 1922, but returned to the Soviet Union at the outbreak of the war in 1939, reconciled on national grounds. She was evacuated from Moscow to the region of Kazan; there, in extreme poverty and ill health, she ended her life by hanging.

page 96. *Lyubka.* This is a popular name for an uncommonly fragrant night violet, a small greenish-white flower found in woods and swampy places. Actually, it is of the orchid species, *orchis moris,* known among the common people as *dremlik* ("the dreamy one").

page 104. *Socialism.* Pasternak was drawn to socialism by its creative forces, as a higher good. To socialism and the distant future he dedicated many poems (*Second Birth,* 1932). He wrote: "With confidence in life as things exist, while facing the future and everyday affairs, one cannot at the end avoid, as in a heresy, an incredible simplicity." He was fascinated by the Revolution and felt himself as its passive victim. Yet the Revolution became to him a sublime reality. He felt it was his duty to bear witness to his times as a poet, not as a camp follower; he refused to surrender to political pressure, to turn his poetry into a vehicle of propaganda. (Putivl in stanza 3 is the name of an ancient town in the region of Sumy, south of Novgorod Seversky; it has reference to the passage in *Lay of Igor's Campaign* in which Queen Yaroslávna laments like a cuckoo the fate of her husband Igor.)

page 116. *Hurry, My Verses, Hurry!* Gogol's "Viy" is the title of a story of romantic weirdness mingled with superstition and ruthless humor.

page 137. *Hamlet.* The title is not a matter of chance or whim. Pasternak understands Hamlet as a drama of duty and self-sacrifice. Hamlet was a man who gave up his own ambitions in order to "do the will of the one that sent him." Through his dead father Hamlet had an intimate personal relationship with Eternity, a relationship between past, present, and future. It was a challenge which he accepted voluntarily as an expression of man's spiritual freedom, as destiny itself. He accepted the bitter cup, as must the poet, the man with a mission and a special responsibility from times immemorial ("The Poet"). Poetry is not merely a craft private in meaning and divorced from man's destiny; it is a means of addressing humanity.

page 143. *Intoxication.* The title in Russian is *khmel'* and the word means both "hops" and "intoxication."

page 147. *August.* The phrase "days of dull despair" (stanza 11) stands for the untranslatable abstract noun *bezvreménshchina,* meaning a state of social apathy, weariness, spiritual letdown, a life without a sense of the timeless. It is a despair which comes from the sin of *acedia,* a sin against love, a kind of sad dejection of mind and spirit ending in despair.